T0128744

MARRIAGE
Minutes

Building a Healthy Marriage
One Minute at a Time

JERRY SHIPP

Marriage and Family Therapist

MARRIAGE MINUTES
BUILDING A HEALTHY MARRIAGE ONE MINUTE AT A TIME

iUniverse books may be ordered through booksellers or by contacting:

iUniverse
1663 Liberty Drive
Bloomington, IN 47403
www.iuniverse.com
1-800-Authors (1-800-288-4677)

ISBN: 978-1-4917-7943-9 (sc)
ISBN: 978-1-4917-7944-6 (e)

Library of Congress Control Number: 2015953734

Print information available on the last page.

iUniverse rev. date: 10/19/2015

Foreword

My friend Jerry Shipp is giving couples a unique approach to help them conquer the challenge of a long, victorious marriage. This is not, as you may expect, just another book-length sermon about relationships. Instead, each chapter features a vivid snapshot of married life. You will see yourself and your spouse in many, if not most of them.

Sometimes Jerry just helps us to laugh at the absurdities of our humanity, and in that laughter we find forgiveness for ourselves and our spouses. More often, and more importantly, he shows us a path through the tangle of old habits and old hurts to find joy again, and to give it.

As a minister I have been permitted to share drafts of these wonderfully pithy observations with other married friends, and the verdict is unanimous: "I loved it!" Every minister and counselor should have a copy to keep and a copy to lend.

Jerry has many years of experience as a marriage and family counselor. He has also "walked the talk" as a husband and a father. He has lived the ups and downs of his own journey as an "open book," and so it's about time he wrote one!

Come along for an engaging ride as, with wit and good will, Jerry leads us through that most maddening, fulfilling and joyful of journeys—a committed marriage.

Randy Daw, Minister
Greenville, Texas
June, 2015

Contents

Major League Marriage

Acknowledgments

First and foremost I want to thank God for being gracious to me. It is only by the grace of God that I have been saved from my sins and from my own devices, not to mention my own doofusness (see MM #49).

God has also blessed me with my wife of thirty years. Gina has been my companion, friend, lover, and co-wayfarer on our journey through life. She is the "iron" that sharpens me. Most recently, she has become an excellent co-therapist as we counsel married couples together. She brings a special softness and a woman's perspective to counseling that I never had in my previous years as a therapist. It is fitting that she has written one of these Marriage Minutes herself and contributed to most of them.

My thanks go out also to Donnie Smith, our senior pastor at The Fellowship. His wisdom, encouragement, and support for this project have been monumental.

I also want to thank Glover Shipp (my dad). He has been my inspiration and the standard by which I have measured success in many areas of my life. He has set the bar high and at 87 is still teaching, writing, composing, and painting.

A big thank you goes to Dr. Libby Weed who did a detailed edit of the manuscript. What a difference it makes getting all the little things, like punctuation and grammar, improved to a professional level.

Thanks go to Randy Daw (friend, minister, and amazing composer) for his comments and ideas. Randy was the first to use a Marriage Minute in his church bulletin.

Thank you to Dr. Jack Tallman, who encouraged me to write, to finish writing, and then held me accountable.

And thanks to Paul Tsika (author, counselor, and pastor) for reading the manuscript and encouraging me to pursue its publication.

May God bless you all with ridiculously long lives.

Introduction

"Marriage Minutes" are exactly that—brief essays that take only a couple of minutes to read that address the challenges we face every day in our marriages. Most of us are so busy that we don't have time to sit down and read a 300-page academic treatise on marriage. We are leery of consulting women's magazines for marital advice. How many times have we seen articles entitled "Three things you can do to make your husband happy" or "The 10 things your wife most wants in the bedroom"? We don't need counseling that badly, do we? After all, good therapists are hard to find. What's a guy (or girl) to do?

Marriage Minutes is an attempt to resolve that dilemma. Humorous and insightful glimpses into modern-day life that are easy to read, interesting, and short! I have drawn from my thirty years of experience as a marriage therapist, and have condensed what I have learned into bite-sized chunks of practical wisdom.

This book is unapologetically written for a Christian audience, although the principles apply to all marriages. You will find old-fashioned, common-sense truth packaged and presented in new ways. It is not designed to be read in one sitting. Read one Marriage Minute. If it fits, apply it. If it doesn't, then put it in your quiver of resources in case you need it later.

Marriage Minutes was written over the course of a year (2013-2014) and first appeared as a weekly blog on the website for The Fellowship church in Round Rock, Texas. It was originally intended to be a set of short videos, and was written in a more conversational style than most articles or blog posts. It became obvious right away that creating more than fifty videos would be a logistical nightmare, so we abandoned that idea. I have attempted to retain the informal conversational tone and I hope that comes through.

I have cited all quotes and references as best I can. If I have inadvertently borrowed from you, I ask your forgiveness because it is too late to ask for permission. If, however, I have been using or adapting your quote for more than ten years, I claim it as my own. If I have misquoted your favorite aphorism, it was probably on purpose. Please forgive me anyway.

I hope that that you find these "Minutes" helpful and inspirational. I also hope that they motivate you to create a great marriage.

To God be the glory!

Jerry Shipp
Round Rock, Texas
September, 2015

In the Beginning: Adam

Let's start at the beginning—literally.

Adam was lonely.

Don't get me wrong. He had all the pets in the world. He had a "man cave" tricked out with the latest devices. He had all the food he could ever want. If it grew on a tree or a bush, it was his to eat, and he didn't have to stand in line at the grocery store.

He had satisfying work—naming all the animals and picking up trash around the garden. Everybody respected him. He had no worries, no fears, no deadlines, and the Boss was his best friend. He could take a day off any time he wanted. In fact, you couldn't really call it "work" in the first place.

It was … Paradise! Everything a guy needs, right? Except football, of course, which wouldn't be invented for a few thousand years.

Life was perfect, except that Adam was still lonely. He had lots of buddies—"lions and tigers and bears, oh my"—but he did **not** have a *companion*. He needed someone with whom he could easily relate, but who was different enough to be interesting and maybe even a little "mysterious."

He began to think about what it would be like to have someone just like him to talk to. The animals all had their mates, their counterparts, but he had no one.

He really did enjoy walking around the Garden talking with God, skipping stones across the pond, catching (and releasing) a few fish, and playing catch with ripe oranges, but it just felt like something was missing.

One afternoon Adam woke up from a nap (Yes, he invented the siesta, and he didn't think the Boss was watching.) and **ZAP!** There she was. God had created Eve and marriage all at the same time!

She was useful. She could actually talk, and she was beautiful! **WOW! Thank you, God!** She was so much fun and she was curious—always asking questions about things. She made Adam feel really smart.

When he looked at her, strange things started to happen to his insides. He would get funny feelings in the pit of his stomach. She made him feel complete (maybe a little nauseous, too, but it was the "good" kind of nauseous). She was a real Godsend!

Those first few days and weeks together were simply amazing. He had never experienced such things before. They spent every minute of every day together. He showed her around the garden, taught her the names of all the animals. Every minute with her was sheer delight.

Then … well, the story gets a little complicated after that, but we will come back to that later.

What a great beginning! Don't you wish you could have started out in Paradise married to the most beautiful (only) woman in the world?

Okay, all you "Adams" out there (yes, I am talking to you), don't forget how empty your life was before *your* Eve burst upon the scene—the joy, the delight, the wonder at how someone so beautiful and amazing would want to be with *you*! Tell her every day that you thank God for her. Tell her how beautiful and alluring she is, and how lonely you would be without her.

And you Eves, do you remember what it was like before careers and children and chores cluttered your life, when the two of you would just sit and talk for hours (or just listen to each other breathe on the phone)? Do you miss the closeness? Tell him every day how wonderful he is and how much you respect and love him.

Perhaps God did create a paradise for Adam and Eve to live in, but He has given us the ability to create our own little Garden of Eden within the confines of our own marriage.

"But, how could it be Paradise without football?" you say. Well, keep reading. This book is designed to help remind you of how it was and how it can be again.

You likely won't find anything new or earth-shattering here, just a fresh look (sometimes humorous, sometimes serious) at marriage and how we can restore the excitement of living life together.

Personal prayer:
Lord, in the midst of our busy, chaotic lives help us to recognize that you made us for each other. You intended for us to complete, fulfill, and uplift each other, but mostly to love each other. May we never forget that.

3

Thank God for Marriage

For the first several millennia of man's existence on earth there were no such things as marriages and weddings.

A union was created when two fathers got together and negotiated a business transaction that would benefit both families. It was done for economic, religious, or political reasons. It united influential families and made them wealthier or strategically stronger.

Wives were considered to be property, whose main purpose was to produce male heirs. (Female children were considered a liability and had to come with dowries as incentives for men to take them off their fathers' hands.) Wives were often treated like possessions, doomed to hard work, or were locked up in a remote place where they would not cause trouble.

Rarely was love ever involved in these transactions. In fact, marrying for love is of relatively recent origin (the last few hundred years).

Christian marriage elevated the status of women and of the marriage relationship. Marriage became a spiritual union and not just a business deal. Husbands were told to love their wives and treat them properly (Ephesians 5:25).

In the Catholic Church, marriage is considered a "holy sacrament." Since it is sacred, it falls under the jurisdiction of the church. A priest solemnizes the relationship and blesses it; the church sanctions it, and regulates it, and only the church can end it.

At the Protestant end of the Christian spectrum, a wedding is performed by a minister, vows are exchanged, and the union is blessed by God and the church with the warning, "What therefore God has joined together, let no man separate" (Matthew 19:6 and Mark 10:9, New American Standard Bible).

Husband and wife are equal partners on a spiritual journey together with God.

There is an assault on traditional marriage in America today. As our society has become increasingly more secularized, that which was originally considered sacred has become worldly. Marriage is not respected as a commitment.

Researchers have told us that the divorce rate in America has been over 50% for several decades. I don't know how accurate that figure is, but I do know that healthy, long-term, committed relationships are no longer considered to be the norm.

I read an article during the 2014 Winter Olympics about a 23-year-old athlete who was happily married and had a small child. He and his wife were both Christians. The reporter called this an alternative lifestyle!

Fifty to seventy percent of children in our public schools are from broken or single-parent homes. Many of the couples I have worked with over the last twenty years have never even seen a healthy marriage! How can you duplicate in your own marriage what you have never seen before? When you take God out of marriage (or anything else, like schools or politics), it becomes perverted. And that is precisely what we are seeing in our country today.

I have found that the healthiest, happiest, and most satisfied couples are the ones who follow the biblical model of marriage (commitment with no back doors), whether they are themselves Christians or not.

It works! It is God who sanctifies a marriage, not any branch of the federal or local government.

I thank God that he created marriage and that he wants it to be a reflection of his relationship with us and Christ's relationship with the church. (Read Ephesians 5:25-32.)

He set the bar high because anything less than that is not good for us. It is a distortion. He also knows that we cannot achieve it by ourselves, but he enables and strengthens us.

Our goal should be to set an example for our families, our neighbors, our communities and the world—of how marriage can and should be.

Personal prayer:
Thank you, God, for creating and designing marriage for us. May our marriages bring honor and glory to you. Help us never to become satisfied with an average marriage, but, as a couple, to shine as an example of how wonderful it can be when we do it your way.

No Back Door

"Hotel California"[1] is probably the best known of all the songs recorded by the Eagles. If you listen to the lyrics, it is a very creepy song. My favorite line is "You can check-out any time you like, but you can never leave." Forty years later, the band is still performing this song to live audiences who delight to sing along.

The hotel they are singing about seems like a happy, fun place, but the fact that you can never leave, is a bit disturbing. I think that many people have that same view when it comes to marriage. "Yeah, marriage is nice and all, but what if it doesn't work out and I want to leave? What then?"

And that brings me to the point of this segment.

Airplanes have them. Malls, theaters, office buildings, and arenas have them. Even school buses have them. They are called "emergency exits"—a way to get out of an enclosed place when something bad happens. Most houses and some apartments come equipped with a back door.

Emergency exits and back doors are options, alternative ways of escaping a difficult or dangerous situation. They represent a Plan B. If Dad is watching the front door, maybe I can sneak out the back door.

Back doors imply escapes, shortcuts, or sneaky ways of removing yourself from a situation.

That is all well and good if you are in a movie theater and there is an earthquake or a fire, but not so good if your marriage is falling down around you.

More than anything else, the key to a successful, enduring marriage is **No Back Door.** No Plan B! No Emergency Exit!

Unfortunately, marital discord has been around almost as long as marriage itself. It usually begins about twenty minutes after you say, "I do."

In our culture today there are a lot of back doors. Our society has become accepting of divorce as a legitimate solution to marital difficulties.

The prevailing attitude is that "if things don't work out, we can just get a divorce and try again with someone else."

But if you ask many of the kids who have been devastated by the divorce of their parents, they will tell you that they are not going to get married. Period. Why? Because they don't want divorce to happen to them, so they will just live together! **What?** I know, crazy, huh?

If you go into marriage with a "back door mentality," the time will come when you will *want* to walk through that back door. One reason my parents have been married for 67 years (as of September 2015) is that they had no idea there even was a back door. Yay! I am glad of that.

There were no other options. They *had* to work things out. And they did! That is the key.

So lock the back door. Nail it shut. Brick it up. You have no other option. You chose the person you married for some very good reasons, and those reasons still apply.

Work it out! I have seen couples overcome all kinds of adversity, such as financial disaster, death of a child, unfaithfulness, and addictions, and they did not get a divorce. In fact, their marriage often got stronger. They had to work very hard, but they got through the firestorm together.

Are there times when the marriage cannot be saved? Even Jesus begrudgingly said yes, but only under extreme circumstances and as a last resort. Not for "any and every reason" (Matthew 19:3-9, New International Version).

The only time the word "divorce" should be used by a married couple is early in the marriage to remove it from their vocabulary and to take it off the table as an option.

When divorce is NOT an option, spouses have to:

- get creative in their problem solving,
- work hard together,
- be patient,
- be persistent,
- pray together,
- be willing to change, and
- commit to being a source of blessing, encouragement, grace, and love to their partner.

That's it! That's the bottom line.

Personal prayer:

Lord, there is only one way to fail in marriage and that is to give up and quit. Give me a vision for my marriage so that I can always see it as it <u>can</u> be, not just as it appears to be right now. Please lock the back door. I want no other options.

Marriage Minute #4

Put a Smile on Her Face

Guys, this one is for you. Some of these Marriage Minutes will be for the ladies; most will be for husband and wife. Right now, the spotlight is on husbands.

We have all heard it a thousand times—"If mama isn't happy, nobody's happy." Yes, you know it's true. If your wife is not happy with you, life pretty much stinks. But what can you do? Does it ever seem that no matter what you say or do to make things better, they just get worse? What is the **secret** to a happy wife?

No mystery here. No secret. Put a SMILE on her face!

Here are 5 quick things you can start doing today.

Number One—Study your wife.

> Learn about her—even after the wedding. Get a Ph.D. in Ginaology (or Jenniferology or whatever your wife's name is).
>
> A lot of men enter "marketing mode" when pursuing a prospective mate. You shave, clean yourself up, put on your best clothes, use cologne, talk about interesting things, spend lots of money taking her to nice places, and calling her up to talk on the phone (or just breathe heavily) for hours.
>
> Then, as soon as the wedding is over, you revert to "standard mode" and all that cool stuff that she liked so much disappears because "I'm tired," or "we can't afford it" or

"we're too busy." And you forget. You started out wanting to know everything about her and doing all those little *special* things that made her the envy of all her friends.

Do you know her favorite color of lip gloss? Where does she like to buy shoes? What is her favorite coffee flavor? Do you know where she would like to go instead of going hunting with you? Do you know her dreams and desires?

You *need* to know these things! Find out what delights her. Don't stop doing the things that worked originally. You are *not* that good a catch, you just did a good job of marketing yourself once. Keep doing it and don't ever stop.

Number Two—Give her what *she* wants, not just what appeals to you.

Does she *really* want another small kitchen appliance or a new hammer? A new sound system for your car? You may have to do some research (see #1). Anyone who has ever been sixteen years old knows how to be sneaky. Use this skill to keep her interested.

Number Three—Treat her gently.

Never speak harshly to her. She may be a competitive athlete, a highly successful business woman, a mom, or a cold-hearted and savage Scrabble™ player, but she will *always* respond better to gentleness.

Treat her like you would your own body. Take care of her. (Read Ephesians 5:28 and 29.) The Apostle Paul talks about that. She is precious to you. Treat her as if she were immensely valuable, because she is.

By the way, plying her with chocolates is *not* abusive, even if she is dieting.

Number Four—Say "YES," always! Your answer to her request is always "yes!"

If she asks for a new Ferrari, say "Yes." Do not freak out over this! Just ask her how soon she wants it and how many children she wants to put to work to get it. But the answer is still "yes."

If she decides it is not worth the trade-offs, or to wait until you can pay cash, that's fine.

Let *her* decide. Gentlemen, spoil your wife and discipline your children, **not** the other way around.

Number Five—Talk to her.

Share your dreams, your passions, your heart, just like you did at the beginning, not just your frustrations at work.

It's all about *your* attitude. Spend time with her doing what she wants to do. Anticipate her needs and wants. Let her know she is more important than anything else.

Build a dream you share together and the future will be yours.

If it feels as if most of these points are different ways of saying "I desire to please, serve, and delight you," then you are starting to understand. Besides, who will benefit the most if there is a smile on her face?

Personal prayer:
Lord, you have given me a precious gift. My greatest desire is to serve and please you and my incredible wife. Help me to overcome my weaknesses, fears, and selfish thoughts and actions that would get in the way of that desire. Grow me into the husband she deserves and you desire for me to be.

24-Hour Contracts

Have you seen the movie, "50 First Dates,"[1] with Adam Sandler and Drew Barrymore? I am not a huge fan of romantic comedies, but I really like this one.

It is the story of a young lady (Drew) who sustained a head injury in an auto accident a year or two earlier on her birthday. The accident completely wiped out her short-term memory so that she can no longer recall anything that has happened since that day. In her mind, every morning when she wakes up it is the same day—her birthday. Every day since she returned from the hospital her family and the local Hawaiian residents have gone to great lengths to perfectly re-enact the events of that day. Enter Adam Sandler's character, an outsider who shows up and falls in love with her.

I won't tell you the whole story or how it ends. Suffice it to say that Adam is faced with the challenge of having 24 hours to meet her and make her fall in love with him, and then, do it all over again tomorrow. And *that's* what I love about this movie!

What if you only had 24 hours to make your spouse fall in love with you? What if marriage were a whole lot of one-day contracts? What if you had to behave in such a way today so as to make your partner **want** to renew the contract tomorrow? What kind of impact would that have on your behavior, on how you communicate with your spouse and children, on your attitude?

Think about yesterday. At the end of the day when you were getting ready for bed, did your partner say, "You were an awesome (husband/

wife) today. I am so excited about being married to you. I can't wait to see what tomorrow brings. I definitely want to renew the contract for another day." Or, was it more like, "What a pain in the fanny you were today. I sure hope tomorrow is better." I think you would be a little more deliberate and a lot more careful about what you say and do.

Did you know that in all his 50 years with the Los Angeles Dodgers, Tommy Lasorda never had more than a one-year contract? His contract was renewed every year based on that year's performance, not on what he had done 10 years earlier. He had to earn next year's contract.

If you took your marriage that seriously, if you had to renew your marriage contract every morning based on your performance yesterday, I wonder how many days you would have been married last year. You need to quit looking at your relationship as if it were a multi-year contract in which you could "average out" your behavior over a long period of time. Every thought, every word, every action needs to build up and edify your spouse.

Stop taking your marriage for granted. You may not have a tomorrow. Ask someone who recently lost his or her spouse! You only have today. Use it wisely and deliberately, because you have no guarantee you will still be married tomorrow.

I am not saying that you should bail out of your marriage just because you or your spouse did not quite "hit it out of the park" yesterday. Maybe you should live as if it were up to you to make sure your partner *wants* to "re-up," *wants* to renew the contract for another day.

Try it. You might like it.

Personal prayer:

Lord, you have told us many times that life is short and that all we really have, by your grace, is today. Help us to not squander our days together but to treat each one as if it is our last one. Help us to cherish each day we get to be together.

Humor

A friend of mine from Oregon sent me a cartoon a while back titled "In God's Kitchen"[1]. It was a picture of God sitting on a sofa watching his flat-screen TV. Behind him in the kitchen the heat was on in the oven and smoke was billowing out. An angel arrived, looked in and asked, "What are you cooking?" God answered, "Texas. Why?"

I am not going to compare Central Texas with Phoenix, Arizona, or Death Valley in California, but it does get hot here. In fact, the other day it was about 103 degrees and humid. I had taken a shower after mowing the front yard and was toweling myself off, but soon was drenched in sweat! I told my wife, "I just stepped out of the shower and now I'm dripping wet!" She didn't miss a beat when she responded, "Duh." I quickly tried to take back my statement, but it was too late. We both busted up laughing.

We enjoy laughing together, and we enjoy laughing at ourselves. I wish I could say that it has always been that way, but that would not be true. We have had periods in our marriage when we could not find much to laugh about. But we have learned that laughter and a good sense of humor are very powerful forces to change both our outlook and our experience. They change our attitude and lift our spirits.

A few weeks ago we were out and about running errands, joking around, and having a good time with each other, when the young man behind the counter said, "You two really enjoy being together, don't you?" I hadn't really thought about it, but he was right. What an amazing thing to say about our marriage, especially coming from a complete stranger!

If you do not have a sense of humor, figure out how to get one. Without it, you may be damaging your relationship unnecessarily. Maybe you are like I was years ago—someone who took everything much too seriously. I was extremely sensitive to perceived criticism, especially from my wife, Gina. Over the years she has learned that if she makes a statement and then smiles and laughs, I immediately relax and do not get defensive.

If you are touchy or hypersensitive, you may both need to— LIGHTEN UP! It's not as if God put you in charge!

Just kidding! God probably did put you in charge. He just didn't tell any of the rest of us.

One of the first families I met with as a young therapist was a lawyer, his wife, and their two teenage kids. They were uptight, stressed out, and fought daily. There was no humor at all. I prescribed a family pillow fight!

What a difference when they came back the next week! They were relaxed, laughing, and enjoying each other. They had spent twenty minutes one day beating the snot out of each other with pillows. Their defenses came down, and for the first time in many years they could relax and be real with each other. Healing had begun.

Laughing and joking around with each other may sound like a pretty simplistic answer, but it really can make a difference. Studies have shown that couples (and families) that spend time playing and laughing together have fewer fights and resolve conflict more quickly.

Can a sense of humor fix everything that's wrong with your marriage? Not everything, but it will certainly change your attitude, and it probably won't cause more damage.

I don't think any marriage ever died from having too much healthy fun together.

Learn some jokes, share funny stories, look for the humor in everyday situations. (Most comedians get laughs by exaggerating common, everyday life experiences such as childbirth and going to the dentist.) But most important of all, learn to laugh at yourself!

Go out there and have a little fun. Laugh at life and maybe even joke around with God a little bit. God does have a sense of humor, you know. Just ask a platypus.

Personal prayer:
Lord, thank you for inventing laughter and displaying your sense of humor in the world around me. Help me not to take myself so seriously that I miss the hilarity of my own quirks and eccentricities. Give me the courage to laugh at myself daily.

Fences

We live next to a greenspace. In Texas, that means that on the other side of our backyard fence you can find a lot of prickly pear cactus, weeds (all varieties), oak trees, mountain junipers (cedars), and "critters" (rabbits, deer, raccoons, scorpions, feral cats, and snakes).

Until our Golden Retriever passed away last year, the critters stayed on their side of the fence. Since then, the fence is more of a formality than a barrier.

A windstorm blew through our neighborhood about eighteen months ago and knocked down part of the fence. This confused our neighbor's little "yip-yip" dogs who started doing their business in our yard. We got the fence fixed right away. I like fences and big dogs that protect the sanctity of our backyard.

Fences are boundaries.

A boundary is anything that defines the limits or extent of something. My skin and hair define the limit of the physical me. My fence defines the limit of my property. It also defines what is not me or mine, that is, anything on the other side of the boundary. There are all kinds of boundaries—personal boundaries, geo-political boundaries, physical and metaphysical boundaries, geographical, social, and legal boundaries.

Boundaries limit behavior. Rules and laws are boundaries that define appropriate behavior and limit reckless behavior. There are consequences for violating laws, especially laws of physics. Ignorance of a particular law of physics does not minimize its effects.

For example, if you are unaware of the law of gravity, you are not exempt from the consequences of violating it. If you step off the roof, you will fall *every* time.

Boundaries limit access. Cities used to have walls to keep undesirables or enemies out. Doors, locks, and gates are means of granting access to those to whom you want to grant access. International geo-political boundaries are imaginary lines that non-citizens used to honor. A boundary that is not enforced is no boundary at all. My dog died and no longer guards my backyard, hence critters.

Man-made boundaries are designed to protect what is valuable or important to us. It is unlikely you will ever waste time or energy protecting something you do not value.

If you own 100 acres of sand and rocks in the Mojave Desert, you are unlikely to ever build a fence around your property. Why? There's nothing of value there to protect. But if you discover a ten pound gold nugget buried on *your* 100 acres, you will construct a twelve-foot high fence with concertina wire on top, guard towers at the corners, cameras and lights everywhere. You will probably buy up all the lots around it as well.

There are two rules in boundary setting:

1. **You will only protect what is valuable to you.** The more valuable it is, the more resources (time, money, energy) you will spend protecting it.

2. **You will not set a boundary that you are either unwilling or unable to defend**.

What about healthy boundaries in marriage?

Before you two can become one, you must first be two. It takes two or more distinct individuals to come together to create a team. Each member brings his or her own individuality, differences, strengths, and personality to the team, for the betterment of all.

You also bring your flaws, weaknesses, failures, and short-comings to the team.

In football, the purpose of the defensive unit is to prevent the other team's offense from scoring touchdowns. Each player must fulfill his uniquely assigned position on the team for the whole team to be successful. Each has a different function, but *all* are necessary. Fielding eleven quarterbacks at the same time will not score many points!

If you do not first recognize who you are, as an individual, and what you may contribute to the relationship, it is unlikely that you will have a good sense of *self*. You may not see yourself as an individual, but more as an extension of your partner. You may perceive that you have no identity of your own, no autonomy, no role, and no value, except for what you derive from your partner.

The only time that degree of enmeshment should even be possible is in the womb, but even there the baby may assert its own individuality. Ask any woman who is seven months pregnant!

It is only when the two of you join together, not sacrificing your individuality, but synchronizing with each other, that you truly become one unit. One heart beating in two chests, you are united in purpose. Synergy is created. You become smarter than the sum of your IQs.

This is marriage at its best. Anything less than this is unhealthy and not aligned with God's plan.

Know who you are and who you are not, because that is the best of what you bring to the marriage.

Personal prayer:
Lord, you have created me a distinctly unique individual according to your design and plan. You have created my partner similarly, but uniquely different in his or her own way. May I always cherish and respect our similarities and our differences. You have made us, together, a unique and powerful team.

Drift

Let's talk about "drift." When you think of the word "drift," what comes to mind? Clouds drifting across the sky? A tired person drifting off to sleep? On a grander scale, maybe you think of continental drift, or perhaps your thoughts drifting aimlessly from one topic to the next, or a boat drifting lazily down a stream?

Whatever visual image comes to mind, we are talking about a slow, gradual movement away from something or someone. Drift is natural. The 2nd Law of Thermodynamics says that drift (entropy) is inevitable. The only way to prevent it or reverse it is to introduce new energy into the system. It takes energy to grow and progress and keep things together.

When drift happens to continents, it is so gradual that we rarely notice that the land is moving, unless you live on the San Andreas fault in California and have experienced a couple of 6.0 earthquakes. Cataclysmic events occur when pressure builds up over a long time and has been confined or compressed.

That is what happens to many marriages—pressure builds up, becomes confined and compressed, and eventually gets released with cataclysmic results. The impact can be devastating. Usually we don't notice the subtle changes or see the pressure building. Devastation in marriage does not come about suddenly or "out of the blue."

There are two ways in which "drift" causes damage in marriage. The first is the result of slow, gradual changes, often due to neglect, laziness, inattentiveness, or **SUD's (Seemingly Unimportant**

Decisions). It is the little things that pile up—one bad habit, one unwise choice, one degree off "true north." One urban legend says that NASA once launched a Mars probe, but the trajectory was based on yards instead of meters. It wasn't off by much, maybe only one or two percent, but it did not come even close to its destination.

If you do not invest time, effort, and resources into your new car, in the form of gas, oil, fluids, tune-ups, and new tires, it will deteriorate and, eventually, quit working altogether. The same thing will happen to your marriage.

For most of us, the biggest cause of neglect is "busyness." We are "too busy" with our careers, driving our children all over the state for athletic events, socializing, working out, and barbecuing with the neighbors. We don't take time to devote to each other, so we fall into bed exhausted each night and wonder why we do not feel close. And so it goes. Drift. It's natural.

Your marriage will not die overnight, just like your car. But, if you neglect it, it will die eventually.

To prevent neglect in your marriage due to "busyness," you must commit each day to investing time and energy into it. Do not forget the 2nd Law of Thermodynamics. If you do not keep putting energy into it, it will gradually slow to a stop! You must close the gaps that sometimes occur from spending eight to twelve hours a day apart from each other. Intimacy must be created and maintained daily.

Pay attention. Be aware of drift! A healthy, happy, intimate marriage is no accident. You don't wind it up like a toy on your wedding day and expect it to keep going for 50 years. It takes deliberate effort on your part to keep it moving forward. But, oh my, is it worth it!

Personal prayer:
Lord, help us to recognize the little things that cause us to slowly drift apart one inch at a time. Give us the courage, strength, and determination to close that gap every day and not let neglect of our marriage allow it to come back.

Trust Fall

Imagine yourself standing on a two-foot square platform, four feet off the ground. Behind you are eight strangers with their arms interlocked ready to catch you, and all you have to do is ... fall. Does the very thought of this thrill your soul and get your adrenaline pumping with excitement? Or, does it terrify you and make you want to crawl deeper under the covers?

Welcome to the trust fall. This is probably my favorite challenge course event as an instructor. The trust fall stirs up more fear and anxiety than any other event. It reveals so much about the participant and never fails to bring up strong emotional reactions.

I routinely tell fallers, "Your only job is to make yourself *easy* to catch. Put your hands in your pockets, lock your knees and shoulders, and head back." **It is all about letting go and trusting someone else to be in control!**

What is it about standing stiffly and falling over backwards that is so difficult? In twenty-five years and thousands of participants we have only dropped one person!

It is amazing how often someone will look to make sure everyone is in place to catch, re-arrange the catchers, then check them again to make sure they didn't leave, and still cannot let go of the fear.

Fear of falling is one of the top two or three fears that people have. It ranks right up there with public speaking and dying! I guess it is so scary because when we are falling, we feel that our life is completely out of control, and most of us do not like that.

Once you pass the "point of no return," it is too late to change your mind. You cannot "catch" yourself. You **have** to trust the people waiting to catch you.

I have seen people who, after finally deciding to fall, forget everything I said about staying stiff and keeping hands in pockets. They gyrate, twist, bend in half, and fling their arms out in a futile attempt to save themselves. All they wind up doing is making themselves harder to catch or whacking a catcher in the noggin.

For some people, letting go is very difficult.

Control freaks make the worst fallers. The worst control freaks are the ones who cannot trust others to do anything. They always have to be in charge. They are the micro-managers of life. They fear that if they are not in complete control of all aspects of their life and those around them, disastrous things will happen.

The same thing goes for relationships. Without mutual trust it is impossible to have an intimate relationship.

Marriage is the ultimate trust fall. We even call it "falling in love." It is exciting, exhilarating, an adrenaline rush, and a thrill ride! And it *is*, at least initially. But, those thrilling feelings cannot last forever; they must change and grow into a permanent, loving relationship. That can only happen where there has been a consistent record of safe catches over a period of time.

Being dropped every tenth time in a marriage is not good enough. Sorry, ninety percent is an F when it comes to your spouse's trust. In baseball, getting a *hit* three times out of every ten at-bats may get you into the Hall of Fame, but not the Marriage Hall of Fame.

For many of us, our inability to trust others has come as a result of abuse or bullying we experienced in childhood. For others, it may be the result of loss, hurt, disappointment, or failure we encountered as a teenager or adult.

How do you overcome those fears when life has taught you that it is not safe to trust others? (If you have suffered as an adult because of trauma from your past, take the time to get professional help.)

When I ask people, "What is the opposite of fear?" most of them say *courage* or *bravery*. But that is not precisely true. You can experience fear and courage at the same time. Fear and courage can exist in the same mind at the same time! In fact, courage is doing what is right or difficult—in spite of the fear!

The Apostle John says that the opposite of fear is love. "Perfect love casts out fear" (1 John 4:18, English Standard Version). Fear and love cannot co-exist! It is not possible to truly love someone and fear them at the same time.

If you have trouble trusting others because of fear, then focus on loving them more, not on controlling them more. Decide to love. Decide to trust.

So, lock your knees, chin up, shoulders back, let go, and enjoy the ride!

Personal prayer:
Lord, help me give up the illusion that I am in control of the events in my life. Help me to face the scary challenges in my life with love rather than fear, and to trust you to catch me and keep me safe. Help me to be vigilant and trustworthy as I catch others who may be falling.

Selfie Sticks and Sacrifice

A young man was hiking in the mountains and saw a bear approaching. Instead of getting the heck out of there as any sane person would do, he turned his back to the predator, took out his cell phone, and tried to take a picture of himself and the bear. He tried to capture an exciting moment in real time; he wanted a selfie that would make all his friends jealous.

That turned out to be a fatal mistake.

It was inevitable. Your arms are only so long, and there are so many friends and background action that you want to capture with your smartphone. What *will* you do?

Voilà! Enter the "Selfie Stick." Extend your reach by three feet and suddenly you are a social networking hero. Everybody wants you to send them a copy. After almost 200 years of photography, the photographer finally gets to be in the center of the picture.

How exciting!

I don't know if anyone has fallen over the edge of the Grand Canyon, Half Dome, or Niagara Falls in pursuit of the ultimate selfie, but I wouldn't be surprised. I am not really interested in being in the same photo as a cobra or an alligator. And sharing a picture frame with a grizzly bear? No, thanks.

So, what is going on here? The Millennial generation has gotten a reputation for being self-absorbed and entitled, but I do not believe they are any more self-centered than previous generations. They have just grown up with technology that I didn't have. I can remember Baby Boomers and Gen Xers being accused of the same thing.

We all want to be the center of attention. "Watch me, Daddy. Look at what I can do." It is our nature to think of ourselves first. It is normal to look out for ourselves. In fact, it's a pretty good idea. It is a survival instinct. A little healthy self-preservation is designed to keep us safe and alive.

In a world in which most of do not have to struggle to survive, that self-preservation instinct has the potential to turn in unhealthy directions. We have a home, a bed, plenty of food and water, clothes, and lots of high-tech toys. But it is never enough.

Start with four cups of technology, add two teaspoons of drama, a dash of envy, a half cup of immaturity, let it boil for a few commercials, and what do you have? "I'll just *die* if I don't get the newest _____."

Suddenly, we have a freshly-baked batch of selfish brownies.

Left uncontested, this selfishness can grow into a need to:

1. be the center of attention and conversation *always*,
2. be loved by everyone all the time, or
3. insist that no one is ever allowed to disagree with you.

What began as a normal instinct to survive has morphed into full-fledged narcissism.

If either you or your partner brings this faulty belief system into your marriage, you are setting the stage for a tumultuous relationship.

Love, intimacy, vulnerability, even marriage itself, cannot function properly in the presence of selfishness, self-indulgence, or narcissism. These three character flaws each insist that "my needs (wants, wishes, desires, preferences, fantasies, goals, priorities) are more important than yours. If you and your petty needs get in the way of me getting what I want, then you have become my enemy."

Do you know someone like that?

Sadly, I have observed this scenario played out hundreds of times in counseling with couples. Most of the time, it ends in either divorce or a long-term, abusive relationship.

The solution to this dilemma is quite simple, though not at all easy. God calls us to a higher level of belief and behavior. He calls us to self-sacrifice, and then steps out of eternity to show us how to do it. (Read Matthew, Mark, Luke, and John for the full story.)

Sacrifice is the only way to make a marriage (or parenting) work. Anything less will fail. Sacrifice says:

1. You first.
2. How can I meet your needs?
3. I will never forsake you or leave you.
4. I will always accept you as you are.
5. I will protect you and provide for you, no matter the circumstances.
6. I will love you always and more than *anything*!
7. I will stand between you and danger.
8. I will die for you.

Does this sound like marriage vows? I would hope so. Have you forgotten the promises you made on your wedding day? This is how it is *supposed* to be. It is what God did because of his love for us. It is how we are to act toward our partners and our children.

Self vs. Sacrifice

Not self-indulgence, but self-denial.
Not selfish ambition, but self-sacrifice.
Not by being first, but being last.
Not lording it over others, but serving them.
Not puffing up yourself at the expense of others, but encouraging and lifting them up.
Not demanding love, attention, or sex, but creating an environment in which love and intimacy can flow freely (read 1 Corinthians 13).

God is love and his love is an inexhaustible resource. It flows through our lives when we love sacrificially.

That's it. That's the only way.

Personal prayer:
Lord, you have shown me what it means to love and to sacrifice. May I never put myself ahead of my spouse or ahead of you. May I be a living sacrifice for my spouse and my family every day.

Dandelions

I hate dandelions! I hate them so much that I have been known to weed my neighbor's lawn and to go around with my "dandelion knife" leaving behind piles of uprooted weeds as a warning to other dandelions not to grow there.

I haven't always hated dandelions. When I was a kid, I used to pick the stems and blow the tufts of white seeds all over the yard. I loved to watch them fly through the air. But now my response when I see someone doing that is, "Nooooo! That's a hundred more dandelions I will have to pull out of my lawn."

Dandelions take over. They choke out the grass. They are probably drought-resistant. If you try to mow them down or pull the tops off, they just grow back bigger. You have to pull out the entire taproot or it will keep growing back.

Once upon a time, I had a weed-free lawn for three whole days! Sigh … It does not take any effort to grow weeds.

We lived in Oregon for twenty years and discovered that it is almost impossible *not* to grow things. In fact, if you do *nothing* to your garden after planting the seeds, you will not get many veggies, but you will get some amazing weeds! But if you want to grow a beautiful and productive vegetable garden, you have to spend time pulling the weeds.

I believe that one reason the divorce rate is so high in our country is because we do not spend enough time pulling the weeds out of our marriages.

Weeds grow naturally. Part of Adam's curse was having to deal with weeds. He just didn't know they would grow in his marriage, too.

What are some of the weeds that spring up in our relationships? Some of these are more than just weeds, they are marriage killers!

- Hurt
- Disappointment
- Anger
- Lack of Forgiveness/ Inability to Forgive
- Selfishness
- Addictions
- Fear
- Unmet needs
- Unrealistic Expectations

It is unlikely you will ever completely eliminate weeds from your life, but there are some things you can do to reduce their abundance and level of destructiveness.

1. **Aerate the soil.** In the case of marriage, that means **communicate!** Maximize your time and effort seeking clarity and understanding.
2. **Fertilize the garden.** That does not mean "throw manure around." It means "feed the good things" in the relationship. Be nurturing. Give it what it needs to grow and be healthy.
3. **Pull the weeds by hand!** There is no easy way and there are no short cuts. Eliminate all negative behaviors, character flaws, and bad attitudes. Get rid of everything that is

choking your marriage—carefully, one at a time. It is a sweaty, laborious job.

4. **You must pull your own weeds.** It is not helpful to point out the nasty weeds in your partner's lawn. The job cannot be delegated. You must do it yourself.

5. **Hire professional weed exterminators.** Sometimes we need help eradicating toxic beliefs and habits. Get professional counseling (if necessary) and spiritual mentoring (always).

6. **Apply pre-emergent before the weeds have a chance to grow.** Eliminate problems before they ever have a chance to take root. Guard your habits. Do not allow negative attitudes or behaviors to become bad habits.

7. **Trust the Master Gardener.** God created marriage and knows what it needs for it to be healthy and strong. Read his guide book for married couples. (You may know it as The Holy Bible.)

Start today. Get out there and pull the weeds that are starting to grow in your own life and in your marriage.

Personal prayer:
Lord, help me to recognize the weeds in my marriage, and give me the tenacity to pull them completely out of my life no matter how painful the process might be. Give me the determination to not give up until there is only your love left in my heart.

Martians and Venusians

Here is something that has been floating around the Internet for a while, attributed to the famous and ubiquitous "A. Nonymous." When you hear these words from your spouse, they may not mean what you think they mean.

Five Deadly Words Used By a Woman[1]

	Statement	True Meaning
1.	"Fine"	Not fine. "I'm right. I'm just going to stop arguing."
2.	"Nothing"	This definitely means **something**, and you should be worried. Arguments that begin with "Nothing" usually end in "Fine."
3.	"Go ahead"	This is a dare, not permission.
4.	"Whatever"	Does the phrase, "go jump in a lake" still have meaning? It's the nicest translation I could think of.
5.	"That's okay"	Not okay. I am deciding how and when you will pay for your mistake.
Bonus:	"Wow!"	"Can anyone really be that stupid?"

Thanks for playing. Anyone get "wowed" lately? The other day I got "wowed" twice in rapid succession.

I have known for a long time that men and women communicate differently. We may use the same words and both think we are speaking the same language, but that is not necessarily true. Just because a word sounds familiar, is not a guarantee that the other person means the same thing when using it.

Dr. John Gray points out in his book, *Men Are from Mars and Women Are from Venus*[2], that men and women think differently, communicate differently, perceive the world differently, react differently, feel differently, and have a very different approach to life and relationships.

Is it possible that we really are from two different planets? Perhaps we are two different species. It's amazing we can relate at all, let alone actually understand each other.

If we are going to stay married and achieve any kind of happiness or satisfaction, we are going to have to learn each other's language. Like the original Rosetta Stone that was the key to translating Egyptian hieroglyphs in the 1890s, we need some kind of decoding device that will translate accurately and precisely into the Martian language what these Venusians are really saying!

As it turns out, there is such a device. In fact, it is a single code word that is the clue for interpreting all Venusian speech.

And the secret code word for Venusians is … wait for it … **relationship**!

(Martian language is more literal, linear, logical, fact-oriented, just so you know.)

Are you shocked and confused by this revelation, or is this a "duh" moment for you? Not being one to exaggerate (cough, cough), I would say that 95-98% of what women say and feel can best be understood when interpreted through the filter of personal relationships.

When I was in graduate school, I learned two rules of communication:

1. **You cannot _not_ communicate.** You may stop talking, but you are still communicating (body language, facial expressions, and monosyllabic guttural utterances), and
2. **All** communication is a commentary on the status of the relationship.

Notice the difference between these two next statements in terms of what they tell you about the current status of your relationship.

"WHAT ON EARTH DO YOU THINK YOU ARE DOING??!!!" vs. "Hey, honey, what are you up to?"

I know it's a subtle difference, but trust me on this. It is the same request for information, but two totally different comments on the status of the relationship.

Because most women tend to be more relational, they are more tuned in to the nuances of communication and its direct impact on the quality of the relationship. Their emotional well-being depends on it.

Ladies, forgive me for making gross generalizations about women. I am not a sexist. I happen to think that this relational focus is a very cool trait and one that does not come naturally to most men.

In fact, while he is struggling to learn the Venusian dialect, you might want to learn a little bit of Martian as well.

Gentlemen, here is the question you should be asking yourself: "What does her statement or behavior mean **in the context of our relationship?**" or, "What does *my* last statement or behavior really say about the status of our relationship?"

If you do this, I guarantee you will be right at least 90% of the time. You may also find that you get "wowed" a little less often.

Personal Prayer:
Lord, give me ears to hear and a will to understand what my spouse is truly communicating, though it may be shrouded in analogies, emotions, or innuendo. Help me to hear past the "noise" to the true meaning of his/her heart.

Minions

What is bright yellow, has one or two eyes, wears overalls, and is shaped like a medication capsule?

A Minion, of course.

Minions are a horde of miniature, bumbling animated characters who serve the evil genius, Gru, in Disney's *Despicable Me*[1] and its spin-offs.

They are funny, lovable, and brainless. They are in total awe of their Master and willingly follow his every command (well, sort of). They are enchanted by him, even though Gru is constantly mistreating, controlling, and manipulating them.

These little stalwarts of servitude have come under his spell.

In past centuries, peasants lived in fear that a witch or sorcerer might cast a magic spell or curse upon them. If that happened, they would lose their will and become the spellcaster's minion. They feared being enchanted or "charmed."

In our modern world, supposedly dominated by science and rational thought, the idea of enchantment has been redefined. These words now have positive meanings and have even been used to describe the process of "falling in love." A young man comes under the "spell" of a young woman and is enchanted by her beauty. He starts to behave foolishly and becomes a blubbering idiot.

The amazing thing is that this is actually a *healthy* response, especially when the attraction is mutual. It just *looks* like he is crazy.

If, however, these charms are used for selfish or narcissistic purposes … if the beguiler's agenda is for his or her own benefit rather than for the benefit of the "beguil-ee," we call that manipulation (or worse).

Women tend to be light years ahead of men in this area. Perhaps that is why we refer to them as feminine charms. She is seductive. She speaks in a sultry voice and lures the naïve young man into her sphere of influence to do her bidding. Gotcha.

The Sirens of Greek mythology (Homer's *Odyssey*) sang beautiful, enchanting songs to lure sailors to their death.

This epitomizes what I call the **Law of Non-Reciprocity.** All take and no give.

If you deceive, demand, or take something from someone without giving something back, you are guilty of selfishness, greed, opportunism, or criminal behavior. Your victim may accommodate you for a while, but if the relationship does not eventually even out, the spell you cast will wear off and the person will leave.

So, how do we get someone (spouse or otherwise) to do what we want without having to coerce or manipulate them? Is there a substitute for whining and/or begging without being deceptive?

Is there such a thing as "healthy manipulation"? I believe so, yes.

Here are a few ideas on how to manipulate artfully.

1. Romance her with love songs. Every generation has its favorite love songs, whether it is The Righteous Brothers' "Unchained Melody"[2] (1960s), or Chicago's "You're the Inspiration"[3] (1980s), or Whitney Houston's "I Will Always Love You"[4] (1990s). Touch her heart gently.

2. Become really good at identifying, anticipating and meeting his or her most important needs. She might like affection, financial and emotional security, companionship, attention, comfort and praise the best. He might prefer approval, encouragement, respect, appreciation or admiration.

3. Engage in quality time together.

4. Renew your commitment daily.

5. Praise him or her in front of others. Do not miss an opportunity to compliment your spouse in public.

Now, doesn't that feel better than whining, crying, and throwing a fit to get your way?

Minions may serve you well (or not), but there is no substitute for a willing partner who shares your dreams and goals, and with whom you are enchanted.

Personal prayer:
Lord, I have fallen willingly under a love spell cast by my spouse from which I hope never to recover. May I be blessed and honored to love and serve her (or him) unselfishly all of my life as I love and serve you.

Scabs

Have you ever gotten a really big scrape on your body? Maybe it was knees, elbows, back, face?

We called them "raspberries." My favorite way to get a big "raspberry" was by sliding into third base on a dirt infield while wearing shorts.

Ouch! Ya gotta love scraping off the top two or three layers of skin cells!

I can still remember how it felt—carpet burns, road rash, and mom's treatment of antiseptic, a Band-Aid (required), and if I were brave, a kiss on the boo-boo. Then a few days later—a scab!

Did you ever try to pick off a scab before it was ready to fall off on its own?

Ouch, again!

Okay, let's review a little physiology:

Q: What is the purpose of a scab?
A: To protect injured skin, so it can heal without infection.
Q: Do scabs have nerve endings? Can they feel?
A: No. The skin under it may feel the pressure of touch, but the scab helps dull the pain.

One more question. Have you ever had a "**radical closed-chest heartectomy**"? What? You've never heard of it? It is not exactly a common medical diagnosis, but I bet you have had one.

You've had a radical closed-chest heartectomy when someone you care about turns on you and rips your heart right out of your chest (without anesthesia), throws it on the floor, stomps on it a few times, and then shoves it back in your face. (Ah, I can see you nodding your head in recognition.)

Most all of us have had this experience. Some of us may have even performed it on someone else. The universal response to this form of non-medical surgery is to go into self-protection mode and tell yourself, "I will *never* let anyone do that to me again!"

You erect a wall around your heart. You put up barricades. You encase your heart in concrete or armor plate. You grow scabs. It hurts too much! You just want the pain to go away. You are in a vulnerable state in which you want to remove the possibility of ever getting hurt again.

I can guarantee that you *will* be successful at never getting hurt again. You will also be very lonely. It is human nature to focus all of your attention on your hurt and to ignore or become insensitive to pain in the lives of others. Or worse … a heart that is closed off has the potential to unintentionally cause hurt to others.

Scabs cannot feel! That is what makes "hurt people" dangerous.

Depending on just how radical the heartectomy was, it can take up to two years to begin to feel better again and for the scab to fall off your heart. But sometimes you just don't have the luxury of waiting that long. You must take relationship risks and start feeling again before you are completely healed. Your heart might still be hurting and sensitive to touch, but leaving the scab on—in the name of self-protection or caution—will cause it to harden and petrify.

In other words, you just have to rip off the scab, ready or not. That is one of the most difficult things a person can do. It is also one of the smartest things. It is far better to take the risk of getting hurt again, than to shrink your heart in order to minimize your misery. Read The Grinch (MM #27).

What will it look like to remove the scab?

- Read good books and grow internally.
- Repair old relationships and seek new ones.
- Get more involved in social activities.
- Serve other people.
- Learn something new.
- Cast a new vision for your future.
- Spend time with God and in the Word.

This week, let God heal your heart by pouring his inexhaustible love into it. He will enable your heart to grow. He will cherish it and keep it safe, for it is his very own.

May God heal you in all of your broken places.

Personal prayer:
Lord, help me to remove everything from my life that gets in the way of an intimate relationship with you and with others. Help me to trust you with my fears, my hurt, and my brokenness.

Captain Picard and the Universal Translator

Someday I would like to invent my own language. A language in which *I* get to make the rules of grammar, where spelling is easy and punctuation is either unnecessary or is visual and obvious—like emoticons or a symbol for an eye roll. Most importantly, the words would only have *one* meaning, so you would never have to worry about being misunderstood.

Have you ever been misunderstood? Frustrating, wasn't it?

I remember an episode of *Star Trek: Next Generation*[1] in which Captain Jean Luc Picard got marooned on a planet with hostile aliens. The story line was that his Universal Translator, which automatically interpreted every alien language into English, did not function properly. In actuality, it was working just fine. It was translating the words into English, but they did not make any sense. The reason it didn't make sense—this alien language had no verbs!

Imagine trying to communicate without any action words. Picard could hear their words in English, but could make no sense of them. They spoke in word pictures of events from their cultural history. Outside of that context their words had no meaning at all.

What's my point? Simply this*: next to being loved, being understood is the most important thing in relationships!* If we are going to connect with others, we must truly understand what they mean. We must enter *their* world and understand *their* experience which shapes the images and meanings of their words.

We cannot trust someone completely who is not willing to make the effort to understand us.

If I spoke only German and you spoke only Hindi, I could pour my heart out all day long confessing my love for you, and you might think I was swearing at you. We have to speak the same language and understand the *meaning* and *intention* of the words.

Wouldn't it be nice to have some kind of *Intergalactic Love Translator* that would help us to interpret our partner's words accurately?

Captain Picard had to go to great lengths to learn how to communicate with these alien warriors. His survival depended on it. The breakthrough happened when he and the alien leader fought together against a common enemy and had to trust each other for survival.

Their shared experience created a new common history and new reference points they both understood. That is when they truly began to communicate with each other. Only then was a peace between them forged.

This may be one reason why couples who have been together a long time can go through a great deal of the day without saying much. It is not because they are weary of trying and failing (okay, maybe sometimes), but generally because they have shared so many of life experiences together. They don't need as many words to understand each other. They have thousands of common memories and common reference points.

The survival of your marriage and family depends on how well you communicate, and how much effort you are willing to put into truly understanding your spouse and children. As Captain Picard has demonstrated, the best way to do that is by building a history of shared experiences, developing shared goals, and creating a vision for the future of all members of the family.

Do not just listen to your spouse's words this week, but listen to the meaning. Interpret those words through the filter of your *Intergalactic Love Translator*. (You actually do have one—it is your heart. Listen to it first, then to your brain.) You will not be disappointed. Learn to understand your mate, even if he or she uses no verbs!

Personal prayer:
Lord, help me this week to listen to the context and the intention of my spouse's communication and not just to the words I think I hear. Help me to truly understand the meaning and to filter it through a heart of love and acceptance sprinkled with grace.

"Sticks and Stones May Break My Bones"

Apparently, when I was ten or eleven years old, my brother David and I wrote some nasty words on the back wall of a small grocery store in our neighborhood. I say "apparently" because I do not remember doing it.

I do remember getting in trouble, however.

Graffiti art is one thing, but back in the early '60s, you didn't dare say anything like that out loud or write it down for others to see. My, how times have changed! I am constantly astounded by the vulgarities I hear coming out of the mouths of adults and their children.

I have three brothers, all pretty close in age. When we were in junior high and high school, we raised insults and put-downs to an art form. We thought it was hilarious to see who could come up with the funniest insults. David retired from the sport as the reigning champion.

"Sticks and stones may break my bones, but words can never hurt me."

Did your parents or teachers ever tell you this after a classmate or bully had called you a name? Mine did. I suppose it was an attempt to make me feel better. It didn't.

I'm sorry, but that saying is just NOT true. I don't think I believed it then, and I certainly do not believe it now.

Hit me with a stick and in three to six days (or weeks, depending on the size of the stick), I will be all healed up. But hit me in the heart with just the right word, and I may never fully recover. You do not have to read very far in King Solomon's writings (Proverbs and Ecclesiastes) to discover that words have the power to hurt and destroy.

The more intimate the relationship between attacker and victim, the more devastating the impact on the victim. How much more is that true of our marriages—the most intimate and transparent of relationships. A marriage can be utterly destroyed by a steady flow of harsh words.

I did not really discover this truth until I was in college. It was then that I made a decision and a vow. I decided that I *never* wanted to be the cause of someone's emotional hurt or the reason for his or her loss of self-esteem. I established four rules of relationships for myself that I promised I would never violate, *no matter how angry I got.*

Those four rules are simply:

1. No put-downs
2. No name-calling
3. No insults
4. No swearing.

I don't need to spell these out for you. You know exactly what I mean.

For the record, I have kept that promise for more than forty years. Have there ever been thoughts in my head that were trying desperately to escape my mouth? Oh, yes! I have nearly bitten my tongue off trying to keep my mouth closed. But I had made a decision and a promise, and I kept it.

So don't tell me, "I couldn't help it!"

As a husband or wife, father or mother, it is your responsibility to build up and to encourage the people around you, not to tear them down. Do not let your tongue be an instrument of hurt and destruction. Instead, let it be a source of life and hope and wholesomeness.

I challenge you this week to not violate any of these four rules. God bless you.

Personal prayer:
Lord, help me to harness my own tongue. You have given me words that have the power to create or to destroy. Take the stick from my hands and the darts from my tongue. Help me always to speak life and not destruction into the lives of others.

Marriage Minute #17

"I Didn't Mean To"

"Waaah! Mommmmyyyyyyyy! Johnny hit me!"
"I did not!"
"Yes, you did!"
"Did not."
"Did, too."

"Well, I didn't mean to."

"I didn't mean to." How often have we heard that as parents? How often do we say it ourselves? Or perhaps, you have said, "Oops! I take it back. I didn't mean to say that. It was an accident."

It seems that my brothers and I were constantly swinging our arms to see how close we could come without actually hitting each other. Of course, somebody always got hit accidentally. My grandmother, who lived with us throughout my teen years, used to say, "Your freedom to swing your arm ends where my nose begins."

The problem is that we always judge ourselves by our good intentions. (Trust me. My intentions were *always* good, noble, and righteous.) Others will judge us by the *impact* we have on them. Our intentions may have been noble, but we will be judged by others and remembered for how we came across—how we made them feel.

"Two Gun" Crowley, a famous Capone-era gangster and cop killer, said, "Under my coat is a weary heart, but a kind one—one that would do nobody any harm."[1] Even criminals and murderers justify

65

their actions by what may have started out as good intentions. Even ruthless pirates had a code of honor amongst themselves.

Most people do not have evil intentions—selfish, perhaps, but not deliberately malicious. They really do not wish to cause harm.

We have trouble understanding how someone could be hurt when we did not do it on purpose. So we put the blame on them for being "too sensitive." We somehow believe that the damage doesn't count if we didn't mean to do it. And we get very upset when others do not instantly forgive us or, for some inexplicable reason, try to hold us accountable for the unintentional damage we caused.

Being aware of this quirk of human nature is especially important in our marriages, where *everything*, pre-meditated or spontaneous, deliberate or accidental, *is interpreted in the context of its impact on the relationship*. It just so happens that women tend to be better at identifying it than men.

How do you know when you have come across poorly? **Feedback!** When the response you get from the other person is significantly more negative than what you would reasonably expect (given the purity of your motives and the nobility of your intent), be aware that communication has failed.

So, rather than becoming righteously indignant and blaming your partner for misunderstanding you, take responsibility for the failed attempt.

Apologize! Do not accuse your spouse of being touchy or overly-sensitive. Apologizing does not necessarily imply fault. It is admitting that you are sorry that a misunderstanding has occurred and reinforces your commitment to clearing things up and getting the relationship back on track.

At this point in the discussion the relationship can go one of two ways:

1. **Hit the Rewind Button**, engage the Edit and Repair function, then hit the Replay button and heal the damage. Whether you intended to or not, you *did* cause damage. That does not make you a bad person. What you do next, however, may have long-term negative consequences! Or ...

2. **Play the Blame Game**, step on the accelerator and escalate. By the time the Self-Destruct function engages, you will have won the Grand Prize of a Free One-Way Trip to Stupidville (read MM #19)!

Either of you can make a healthy communication choice *at any point in the process* and get off the downward spiral. Choose the line below that best fits your situation.

Mr. Insensitive can say, "I'm sorry. I think that came out wrong. Let me try it again."

Ms. Hyper-sensitive, can say, "I'm sorry. I think I heard you wrong. Why don't you try it again?"

Your assignment this week is to *assume* good intentions on your spouse's part and figure out what he or she really intended to say. Also, increase your awareness of how you actually come across to others. You might be surprised by the outcome.

Personal prayer:
Lord, help me to see clearly how I come across to others, especially to my spouse and children. Create in me an open and contrite spirit and a heart that does not get defensive but seeks to connect. Help me freely admit when I have misunderstood or have communicated poorly.

Godzilla

When I was a kid, my brothers and I loved to watch the old Japanese Godzilla[1] movies. They had everything young boys love—big fire-breathing lizards, lots of explosions, knocking down skyscrapers, and smashing cars and trucks. They were supposed to be scary monster movies, but they were so hokey, we were never scared. (Perhaps a little "concerned" every now and again.)

Usually, by the end of the movie, we were cheering for Godzilla.

It seems, in retrospect, that Godzilla was always angry and it was never clear why. He would just start throwing cars, stepping on people, and knocking over buildings. The story lines were pretty predictable—big, bad lizard destroys Tokyo, but the tiny humans are eventually victorious.

Do you know anyone like Godzilla? Are you married to one? They seem to be angry all the time. It doesn't matter what the circumstances are, they are constantly irritated. Not much fun to live with.

Like the citizens of Tokyo, if you live with a Mr. or Ms. Godzilla, you live in constant fear of getting squashed.

When you get home from work, do you hesitate a moment before going inside and wonder, "Who is going to greet me on the other side of the door? The beautiful princess I married or Mrs. Godzilla?" Or, when your husband pulls into the driveway, do you briefly speculate,

"Who is going to walk through the door—Prince Charming or Mr. Godzilla?"

After a few years of not being able to predict consistently one way or the other, you may find excuses to delay coming home. You may stay late at work unnecessarily or run some errands on the way home in order to delay that inevitable encounter with the unknown.

If you begin to see a consistent pattern of Godzilla-like behavior, your marriage could be in deep trouble!

Do you yell, scream, throw things, break things, create HITWs (holes in the walls), insult your partner, punish your children severely for the slightest infractions, or embarrass your family in public with your rants and tirades?

Late one night I went into a fast-food restaurant in Southern California and saw a man who claimed to work for the health department, screaming at a teenage employee for touching his own nose. The official made a fool of himself and humiliated his wife and children who were cowering at a table in the corner. In his arrogance and anger, he crushed a teenager's spirit.

Being able to anticipate positive, loving interactions with your spouse is essential to a happy and intimate relationship. People who are predictably pleasant will be admired and respected. People who are predictably negative will be avoided.

Unpredictability is abusive. After all, who wants to snuggle up to a porcupine, or to a giant angry lizard? Only another porcupine or giant, angry lizard.

So don't be surprised, Godzilla, if you get home and another Godzilla is there waiting for you. It may be her (or his) way of surviving your anger.

If you have a problem with anger, get help! If other people complain about your anger, whether you believe you have a problem or not, get help anyway. Do *not* become a Godzilla in your own home.

Personal prayer:
Lord, there are so many things in my life that frustrate and anger me. Help me to see the world from your perspective and not take out my anger, frustrations, and failures on those I love the most. Help me become someone who always builds people up rather than tears them down.

Stupidville

I love scales of one to ten.

I love them because there is absolutely nothing scientific about them, and yet everyone uses them and accepts that they are true. Unless it is your current pain level, your golf score, or the Richter Scale, a ten is always really good and a one is really bad.

Whether it is your self-esteem, your feelings, how you liked the movie, your job, your new car, or the ice cream cone you just ate, you can measure it on a scale of one to ten.

Communication is no exception. In this case we will go with the golf score standard—the lower the volume and intensity, the better. So, if we assume that all communication can be measured on a ten-point scale, perhaps it would look like this:

Level 1: Whispers. Private or secret conversations.

Level 2: Normal Conversation. Children do not have a setting for Level One or Two.

Level 3: Salesmen. Any fast-talker with an agenda. Minimal listening.

Level 4: Cheerleaders!! Rah!! Louder and more dramatic, but still positive.

Level 5: Bi-polar. Anger and negativity show up. At this point it can go either way.

Level 6: Land Mines. Watch where you step! "Well, what about the time you …?"

Anything after Level 6 is harmful to the relationship. If you continue to escalate, you will eventually (and it is amazing how *quickly* this can happen) end up in …

Level 7: Stupidville. You will say *anything* to win. Truth and reality are irrelevant.

Level 8: Dead Silence. Words and volume are no longer enough. There is only seething rage.

Level 9: Get Physical. It is at this level that physical assault happens and police get involved.

Level 10: The Nuclear Option. Your lawyers are threatening each other.

Let's focus on Level 7, because that is where most of the relationship damage begins.

You arrive in Stupidville when you angrily say things that you do not mean and that are not even true. You say them because "you hurt me and now I'm gonna hurt you back." Stupidville is about pay back, revenge, and winning at all costs.

There are no resort hotels in Stupidville, no grand vistas, no beautiful scenery. It is not a great place to visit, yet many couples spend considerable time there.

The sad thing is that we do eventually (and it is amazing how *long* this can take) calm down, but we rarely go back and clean up the mess we just made of the relationship. It keeps accumulating until the whole system collapses.

The real challenge with Level 7 is that once we have been there, it takes less time and effort to get back there the next time. Like an earthquake aftershock or the flooding that comes after a storm, the damage becomes even greater. The more often we go there, the more the hurt piles up.

So, how can we avoid taking these excursions to Stupidville?

First of all, keep the conversation positive, even if it is not going well and you are getting frustrated. Being loud and emotional is not necessarily a bad thing, as long as you stay positive.

Next, learn how and when to call a **time-out** (read MM #20).

Escalation increases energy and builds momentum. The farther you go up the scale, the faster you go, the harder it is to stop. It is essential that you stop this runaway train before it gets going too fast.

If you wait until you are at Level 6 before you hit the brakes, you will skid right into Stupidville.

Finally, make sure that you *never* push the ladder higher.

It is human nature to retaliate. If you react to me at a Level 3, I am likely to come back at a 4 because, obviously, you did not hear me correctly. If you had, you would have agreed, so I will make my point louder. Then you come back at a 5, and I raise you to 6.

And so it goes, to Stupidville and beyond.

STOP THE INSANITY!

So, your next assignment is to:

1. Keep it positive.
2. Slow down, stay in control of your tongue, and
3. Never push it to the next level.

By the way, how are you doing on a scale of one to ten?

Personal Prayer:
Lord, may every word that proceeds from my mouth be used to lift up and encourage others, especially the ones I love. May my words never be used to damage others. Help me to trust you to be my source of strength and protection and not rely on my own ability to defend myself at the expense of others.

Time-out

Take your right forearm and hold it perpendicular to the ground with your fingers pointing straight up. Now take your left palm and touch the fingertips of your right hand, forming a "T." You have just called a "time-out."

This hand signal is accepted all over the world as a request to stop the clock. Call for a break so you can talk things over. Stop the action so you can discuss strategy or tend to the injured.

Wouldn't it be great to be able to do that in real life? Call a time-out, catch your breath, assess the situation, and then resume action only when you are ready?

Calling a time-out at the right moment can be a game-changer. You can disrupt your opponent's momentum, psych them out, change the play, or share important information with the other players. The coach can substitute players and give encouragement. If you call a time-out at the wrong time, you can lose momentum and possibly even the game.

While the world of sports is regulated by strict rules of conduct, time clocks, and referees, our relationships are *not*. Saw that one coming didn't you? There are times when you really do need to call a time-out and take a break from the action.

As we discussed earlier (MM #19), you need to slow down and stop escalating, so you don't end up in Stupidville.

So, how do you do this at home with your spouse and children? As you might suspect, I have come up with some guidelines for using time-outs effectively.

1. **Call a time-out before it is too late.** Do not wait until the clock runs out and you are both verbally and emotionally out of control (Level 6 or 7). It is best to call it when you are still rational (Level 3 or 4).

2. **Agree on the signal.** Whether you use the universal time-out signal, pull on your ears, cross your eyes, or stick out your tongue, make sure the other person recognizes it for what it is—a gesture of peace!

3. **Both sides MUST honor the time-out.** Both *must* disengage. It doesn't matter who makes the call. In football, basketball, water polo, or any other sport, one team does not get to keep playing while the other takes a break.

   This is the rule that is most often violated in marriage.

4. **Use it sparingly.** In most sports you are only allowed a few time-outs per game. Do not call a time-out just because you are uncomfortable with the topic of discussion, or every time your spouse disagrees with you. The purpose of the time-out in a relationship is to make sure everyone stays safe. Do not nullify its effectiveness by over-using it.

5. **You must retreat to different rooms** where you cannot see each other for a minimum of 20 minutes. Why? Because that is how long it takes to calm down physiologically when you are hot and bothered. Glaring at your spouse from across the living room won't do it.

6. **You may go outside, but you may not leave the property.** No fair slamming the door in anger and driving away! One person's avoidance behavior might kick-start the other's abandonment issues.

7. **If you need another 20 minutes, take it, but no more than that.** Otherwise, sit back down together (at a Level 2) and continue the discussion.

This technique may sound a little simplistic, but if you do it sincerely and respectfully, it will work.

You will *not* have one winner and one loser. You both will have won the relationship.

Now go out there this week and call time-outs judiciously and strategically. A well-timed time-out can prevent frequent side trips to Stupidville.

Personal Prayer:
Lord, grant me the wisdom to know when I am about to lose control of my tongue and my voice. When I am losing control, give me the self-discipline to call for a break. More than anything, I want to build up my spouse, but sometimes in the heat of battle I forget who the real enemy is—my own selfishness and impatience.

How to Fight Well (Part 1) What's the Point?

I grew up with three younger brothers. I was the oldest, but unfortunately not the biggest. We fought—a lot. I don't know that we ever drew blood or blackened any eyes, but we wrestled and argued constantly. Our fights usually ended when the biggest brother prevailed or three ganged up on one. Sometimes mom or dad called an immediate cessation of hostilities.

I don't think our fighting ever actually resolved anything, but we fought anyway.

We were all very competitive and strong-willed, so compromise was rare. Our fighting was all about winning. We fought like typical boys—exerting physical or verbal superiority, establishing a pecking order, learning what the boundaries were, and competing.

There was usually only one winner and several losers. No win-win situations for us. (That didn't come along until we had all grown up a little.)

The trouble was I didn't win very often. I suppose that fairness would dictate that I only *deserved* to win 25% of the time. But I had seen that number decrease every time another brother was born, from 100% to 50%, then to 33%; and I was not happy with 25%.

A few years later we adopted a baby girl and she won *all* the time. My dream of sibling supremacy was lost forever.

When couples fight, the stakes are vastly higher. If your goal in fighting is to *win* because justice and righteousness are on your side, then you will surely fail and cause damage to your marriage (go back and re-read Stupidville, MM #19).

Conflict *will* occur. Disagreements will happen. On the way to becoming a great couple, you will have the opportunity to overcome great challenges, perhaps even great adversity. The real test of dealing with conflict in your marriage is *who you become in the process*!

The proper end result of fighting in marriage is to come to a greater understanding of each other.

It can be argued that there is no such thing as a *good* fight, but, in my opinion, all you have to do is look at the outcome. A good fight ends up with a lot of kissing and hugging. There may be something to that old idea of kiss and make up.

Whether a fight is helpful or harmful depends on the answer to this question: "Will your relationship be strengthened or damaged; will you grow closer together or farther apart?"

It has very little to do with the topic, but *everything* to do with the relationship! It also requires some finesse. Good finessers recognize that conflict is an indicator that something is amiss. It is an opportunity to learn more about each other, to re-affirm your love and commitment to each other, and to adapt to and serve each other better.

I don't know if it was the result of all our fighting when we were boys, but today my brothers and I have a great relationship. We disagreed over a lot of things, but we knew that we would always be brothers.

Without a deep sense of commitment, any disagreement has the potential to end the relationship. What enables you to grow as a couple is a commitment to resolving the issue.

I do not particularly like conflict. But I am confident that if I am gentle and caring and never harsh or impatient, we will eventually find a way through the problem and our marriage will become stronger. (That's when all the kissing and hugging happens!)

Go out there and show some finesse!

Personal prayer:
Lord, help me to see that winning the argument and winning my partner's heart are two very different things. Help me to see the collisions in my marriage as opportunities to grow by submitting my ego to the higher purpose of understanding and serving my partner better.

How to Fight Well! (Part 2) The Rules of Engagement

I loved watching the old TV show *Get Smart*[1] with Don Adams as Agent 86. It was a spy spoof that epitomized the struggle between the forces of Chaos and Control. They immortalized the "Cone of Silence," the shoe phone, and "Would you believe …?"

Though hilariously inept, the agents of Control somehow always managed to win. It was fun to watch their bumbling attempts at sophistication.

One lesson I learned was that the "good guys" always told the truth and played by the rules, but the "bad guys" always cheated and lied. So if you cheat and lie, you become a bad guy.

Life was much simpler in the mid-60s, but there are some truths there that still apply to us today.

When you are faced with marital conflict, it is important that you always speak the truth and that you abide by unbreakable *rules of engagement*. Adherence to these rules will enable you to get the results we talked about last time (see MM #21) and to create an atmosphere of love, trust, and cooperation.

If you speak the truth lovingly, there is no topic too difficult to address, no matter how bumbling you may be.

Remember that the goal here is greater intimacy! When some people are hurt, angry, disappointed or frustrated, they tend to withdraw and create emotional safety by distancing themselves from their partners.

Below is a brief scale for measuring closeness in resolving differences.

But first—NO TEXTING ALLOWED for conflict resolution. Texting only works when you are already close and there is little chance of misinterpretation. Being cryptic does not work.

Seven Levels of Closeness

Level 1 – **Email or snail mail a letter**. Write down everything you need to say. The advantage here is that you can express yourself without interruption and edit several times before sending it. I *highly* recommend this. They cannot hang up on you and they can read it when they are ready.

Level 2 – **Make a phone call**. Talking to your partner live is always better. However, you may *not* hang up in anger. Hanging up is grandstanding and immature. (Those old phones were great for slamming down, weren't they? I don't recommend it if you have a cell phone.)

Level 3 – **Sit back to back in the same room.** Sometimes people are so upset or hurt that they cannot look at their partners, but still have things they need to say in person.

If you are distracted by your partner or by visual cues, face away from each other.

Level 4 – **Sit face to face across the room.**

Level 5 – **Sit closer or next to each other,** but still beyond physical reach.

Level 6 – **Sit face to face**, holding hands, eyeball to eyeball, speaking gently.

Level 7 – Well, let's just say it involves a lot of non-verbal communication in private.

Okay, now some **Rules of Conduct**.

- **No physical violence**, threats, or intimidation—ever! Not any. NEVER! EVER! Got it?
- **No swearing**, profanity, insults, name-calling, or put-downs. These are the opposites of your goal. They create more damage and distrust, not more understanding and intimacy.
- **Stay on topic.** Do not try to deal with more than one issue at a time.
- **No "gunny-sacking."** Do not save up your backlog of old issues to dump on your partner all at once. That is not about resolution; it is more about revenge.
- **Turn off the TV.** No distractions or feigned indifference. Do not pretend you do not care about the outcome.
- **No yelling!** Cheerleaders can be loud and still be positive. Trust me when I say, "*You* can't." Don't try.

Don't forget the lesson from Maxwell Smart (from *Get Smart*): If you use the same tactics as the bad guys, you become a bad guy.

You must hold yourself to a higher standard. Fight by the rules.

Personal prayer:
Lord, help me to be constantly on guard for how I try to fix things in my relationships. The ends do not justify the means. How I resolve conflict in my marriage *does* matter. Give me the wisdom and the understanding not to make things worse while trying to make them better.

How to Fight Well! (Part 3) Getting Resolution

In previous chapters we have talked about such things as drift, weeds, inertia, Godzilla, and The Second Law of Thermodynamics—and how all of these are analogous to marriage. They are all natural occurrences (okay, not Godzilla). You do not have to go out of your way to make them happen. Weeds grow. Wood rots. Metal rusts. The universe winds down.

In Nature all living things are either growing or dying. There is no "just existing." There is no neutral. Marriage is a living thing; therefore, it too is either growing or dying.

There is no sense of "If I leave it alone or do no deliberate harm, everything will be okay." Sorry, that approach is not going to work. You are either actively strengthening and building the relationship (good), passively letting it die of neglect (bad), or actively harming it (very bad).

There is only one good option here.

Let's take a look at how you can resolve your differences (fight) and strengthen your relationship at the same time.

Here are nine steps that, if you do them consistently, will get you the results you want.

1. **Timing** is absolutely critical. Don't even try to tell me that you don't know when it is not a good time to discuss something important with your partner. Do not bombard him or her as he or she is walking in the door from work, or when there are three kids crying in the bathtub. Wait until he or she is in a proper frame of mind.

2. **Make an appointment.** Schedule the fight. Let your spouse know up front (this is called "front-loading") what you want to talk about (one topic only) and approximately how much of his or her time you need.

   Never ask for more than thirty minutes.

   Then ask when a good time would be to sit down and talk, preferably later today (within 24 hours). *Never* right before bedtime! This gives your partner an idea of what to expect and time to prepare mentally and emotionally. After all, you have been obsessing over it for three days already. Give your partner a little time to prepare. In other words, no sneak attacks.

3. **Listen.** The person who calls the meeting talks first (just because). You may ask what kind of listening is desired. In other words, is this listening for the purpose of seeking solutions, making suggestions, giving advice (unlikely), or just letting you download your emotions?

   Then, **do not interrupt!** The only exception is to ask for clarification if you are confused by what was just said. For example, "I'm sorry. I'm not sure I got that. Can you run it by me again?"

4. **Nod your head** and grunt occasionally. Smile or frown slightly as deemed appropriate. Show signs that you are

tracking with him or her. Do so *until the speaker is done*. (Hint: Get it all said in ten minutes or less. Most people's attention span is not that long.)

5. **Summarize what you have just heard the other say** until he or she agrees that you have understood. This is NOT a debate! Do not launch into a long recitation of the inaccuracy of all the points. When your partner is satisfied that you "get it," it is your turn to ...

6. **Share your feelings,** insights, thoughts, opinions, research, possible solutions (if appropriate), and end with a statement of your commitment to the relationship and to finding resolution.

7. **Negotiate and compromise.** Do not attempt to jump here from #2 or, worse, try to start here. Take turns laying out what all the options and potential solutions could be. No idea is too dumb to be excluded from consideration. That "dumb" idea may stimulate a brilliant solution.

8. **Come to an agreement.** Choose an option, or adjourn to gather more information. If you need to do more research to get more information or more options, give yourselves some specific assignments and agree on a specific time to re-convene and complete the discussion.

9. **Follow through.** Whatever you agree upon *is a binding contract*. You are only responsible for holding up your end of the agreement. If you need to go back and re-negotiate the deal, do so, but only after a new discussion and a new agreement. You may NOT arbitrarily change the deal!

It is a good idea to maintain your sense of humor and your goodwill throughout this process. By that, I do not mean that it is okay to laugh at or make light of something your partner is deadly serious about, but please quit taking everything *so* seriously.

Will this work every time? **YES!**

Will you get your way every time? Absolutely, if *your* way is defined as what you *both* decide is best for your partner, yourself, and the marriage.

Personal prayer:
Lord, you are the source of life for every breathing thing and have given the promise of abundant life for my marriage. You have made my marriage worth fighting for. Help me to not lose sight of the goal—to honor you and to strengthen my marriage, not just to win an argument.

Guaranteed Success

I have an annoying habit.

If your response to this statement is, "Only one?" then you have been talking to Gina.

My idea of "helping with dinner" is putting things away before Gina is done using them. I also have a tendency to clean the countertop right after she has just cleaned it.

I am better than I used to be, but it has not been easy to stop.

I also tend to sneeze uncontrollably, ten to fifteen times in a row (Gina says fifteen to thirty times), but that is momentum, not habit. And she is annoyed by it.

Some people chew their fingernails, some twirl their hair. I used to crack my knuckles when I was a kid. Several adults warned me that I would be sorry some day for doing that, and I am. Some people even chew tobacco. Now that's a nasty habit! (If you chew, don't wait around for an apology, because you are not getting one.) These unhealthy behaviors become bad habits over time.

A habit is a behavior repeated so many times that it becomes automatic.

Many authors, such as Stephen Covey[1], John C. Maxwell[2], and cartoonist Scott Adams[3] (Dilbert), have written about the power of daily habits to determine our effectiveness (or ineffectiveness) in life.

Marriage is a relationship often dominated by habitual ways of responding to each other. Some of those ways are negative and some are positive. The more positive our habits are in marriage, the more satisfying and healthy the marriage will be.

Developing good work habits, thought habits, and relational habits may not guarantee success, but they do make success possible. Many people have said, "The devil is in the details." That may or may not be true, but it is true that success is found in your daily routine.

Here are some daily, weekly, and monthly habits that will help keep your marriage vibrant and healthy:

Daily Habits

1. **Invest 15-30 minutes** twice a day in face-to-face conversation (not about the kids!) This is where you will learn to enjoy each other's company.
2. **Spend 15-30 minutes** in personal growth and development—reading, studying, prayer, etc. This is how you become an interesting person.
3. **Enjoy 15-30 minutes** of non-sexual physical touch. Maintaining physical closeness can be done while doing other things. The more time you spend doing #1, the more time you get to spend doing #3. That is why it is an investment.
4. **Eat** at least one meal together (preferably two) at your own dining room table. Note that this is not listed under Weekly Habits!
5. **Play,** exercise, or recreate together. Minimum **30 minutes,** more on weekends.
6. **Pray together.** Daily! I don't know the statistics, but I can guess that "zero" couples who are separated or divorcing have spent significant time doing this.

Weekly Habits

1. **Go on a date**. It does not have to be exotic or expensive (*52 Dates for You and Your Mate* by Dave & Claudia Arp[4]).
2. **Have sex** once or twice. Twice a month to five times per week is considered the "normal" range for healthy couples (depending on a bazillion other factors). Most men's sexual energy peaks every three days.
3. **Go to church** together one or more times.
4. **Do chores** together. Doing almost anything together will build strong bonds based on shared experience. This is the stuff memories are made of. When your partner is gone, these are the things you will cherish.
5. **Have a manager's meeting.** (This does not include children.) Sit down together and coordinate your schedules for the next week.

Monthly Habits

1. **Evaluate** last month and set new goals for this month.
2. **Schedule a weekend away** for just the two of you some time in the next quarter.
3. **Have a family conference.** Talk about whatever they want.
4. **Spend one to two hours per month** "**dream-building**" or vision-casting. Share your dreams of what you want to accomplish during your life—socially, spiritually, materially, professionally, etc. This gives purpose and direction to your marriage.

These are more like suggestions than laws, but they are the things that will create a legacy for your children to follow.

The Bible warns that the children will be punished (suffer the consequences) for the sins of the parents to the third or fourth generation" (Exodus 20:5, NIV). We have seen this to be true of generational abuse, addictions, divorce, and criminal behavior. It is also true of academic and professional success, life-long marriages, community leadership, and devotion to God.

It all begins with developing healthy habits in our marriages. Keep doing the difficult things until they become natural and automatic. You will create a legacy of success, rather than of failure or sin, for the next three or four generations.

Personal prayer:
Lord, help me to create healthy habits in my marriage and in my home. Thank you for the blessing of home and family and help me never to grow weary of serving those I love the most.

Tarzan and Jane

I loved to watch Johnny Weissmuller as Tarzan[1] on TV when I was growing up. He was "King of the Jungle." He could swing on vines, talk to animals, and ride around on an elephant.

I wasn't sure why he needed a girlfriend, but what a great opening line: "Me, Tarzan; you, Jane."

He already had everything a guy really needed. But I assumed it was because every hero needs a fair damsel to rescue.

It wasn't until many years later that I began to wonder how Tarzan developed any social skills at all, since he was raised by an elephant and a chimpanzee! Now there are two animals not well-known for their emotional sensitivity.

I can just imagine Jane getting a little frustrated six months into their relationship. It might sound a little like this:

Jane: Hey, Chimp Boy!

Tarzan: Me Tarzan.

Jane: Yeah, tell me about it.
          Look, Tarzan, you have got to work on your social skills.

Tarzan: Me not dumb, Jane Porter, just clueless.
          How bad is it?

Jane: 60%, on a good day, Jungle Man. That was a D-minus when I was in school!

Tarzan: Ooh, not good. I will work on it and see what I can do.

Jane: Good thinking, rocket scientist!

Tarzan goes off and gives some thought to the problem of how he can improve his relational skills with Jane and make her happy. He sets a goal, makes a list, takes an online course on "Relationships with American Women (RAW 101), and reads *Everything I Know about Women I Learned in the Jungle.*

Two weeks later he comes back and talks to Jane.

Tarzan: Miss Jane, I am so pleased to see you again. May I offer you a cup of tea?

Jane: Impressive!

Tarzan: What do you think, Jane? How am I doing?

Jane: Better. The orchids are a nice touch, but you need to tuck in your shirt. Shaving once in a while would be really nice, and a little deodorant would work wonders. I give you a C. Definitely a C, maybe a C+, 78%.

Tarzan: OK, I get it. I need to crank it up another couple of notches. I'll see you in a couple of weeks.

Tarzan goes off muttering something about "this is going to be harder than I thought." He applies himself twice as hard and sets a new goal—92%. "That's an A by anyone's standards," he says to himself.

He subscribes to Jungle Gentleman's Fashion Monthly, reads *Proper Etiquette for Jungle Kings* by Emily Mbagwe, watches Dr. Philoz, and writes a treatise, "The Seven Mating Habits of the Sub-Saharan Tsetse Fly," to prove his heightened level of sophistication and his intellectual prowess.

He washes his best loin cloth and puts on some New Spice jasmine-scented deodorant. Just to be on the safe side, he grabs a bottle of freshly squeezed banana/guava/papaya juice and an armful of cymbidiums. "I am *so* ready for this. Won't she be impressed?"

Tarzan: M'lady, you are looking particularly beautiful today. May I treat you to breakfast on the veranda?

Jane: Oh, my goodness. Don't you look good?

Tarzan: Thank you. You are too nice.

After an hour of delightful conversation and a vine-swinging tour of the latest chimpanzee condominium project, Jane is truly impressed.

Tarzan has displayed a new-found wit and has expressed interest in her feelings and aspirations.

Jane: Well, Tarzan, you have really turned things around.

Tarzan: Thank you, Jane. That means a lot to me. What do you think now? Do I get an A?

Jane: Definitely, a solid 95%.

Tarzan: (Pumps his fist in the air.) Yes! I did it! Mission
            accomplished. I can stop now, right?

Jane: What are you talking about?

Tarzan: My goal. I hit it. I got an A, 95%! I can stop now, right?

Jane: Why would you want to stop? I was thinking that since
            you are this close, 98% is very doable.

Tarzan: Nothing I do is ever good enough for you.

All right, so maybe they never had that conversation; but plenty
of other Tarzans and Janes have. The problem is that both have
misunderstood a basic difference between the sexes:

> **Men** are task-oriented. Give him a specific job to do, and
> then praise and reward him when he accomplishes it.

> **Women** are relationship-oriented. Regardless of the situation
> or task, it is the quality and maintenance of the relationship
> that is important.

> They ascribe to the CRI model of marriage—Continuous
> Relationship Improvement. If you *can* improve the
> relationship, why would you *not want to*? It is a never-ending
> process.

For a lot of men that is an overwhelming and horrifying thought,
not to mention a lot of work!

How can we help each other improve and not frustrate or discourage each other in the process? Here are a couple of ideas:

Ladies, give your Tarzan several small relationship tasks (one step at a time) and praise him for his efforts. Be sure to reward him for each positive step along the way.

Make your advice rare, your praise bountiful, and your correction gentle and respectful. Harshness will destroy his motivation, and without motivation, there will be no growth.

Gentlemen, learning, developing, and honing any skill (whether it is fishing, woodworking, or throwing a football) requires many years of practice to become really good. Marriage is no different.

Do you spend more time improving your golf swing than you do your marriage? (Ooh, I bet that hurt.) Allow her to teach you how to relate to her. If you were trained by a chimpanzee or an elephant, get a new coach!

Now, get out there and *improve your marriage, continuously!*

Personal prayer:
Lord, help me to come to terms with my partner, who thinks, sees, feels, and responds differently than I do. Marriage is a growing thing and, therefore, constantly changing. Give me the understanding to anticipate change and the wisdom to prepare for it.

The Key to Prolonging the Fireworks

Back in the late 1980s Jack Nicholson and Bobby McFerrin recorded a wonderful rendition of Rudyard Kipling's "The Elephant's Child."[1] According to the story, elephants did not start out with a long trunk but acquired it in a tug of war with a crocodile.

This happened because of the young elephant's "insatiable curiosities."

In the fable, the young elephant's relatives initially punished him for being curious, but eventually they all set out to get their noses lengthened as well.

Curiosity. What a marvelous thing! Curiosity may not have actually "killed the cat," but it does make life more interesting.

God has given us inquisitive minds. We love to decipher codes, unravel mysteries, expose secrets, and solve riddles. It is what drives us to explore the unknown, cure diseases, and invent new technology. We are constantly seeking out new things to learn and new riddles to solve.

Once we have "cracked the code," we tend to lose interest in a mystery and move on to the next one.

For good or for ill, this also applies to marriage. For most couples, the most exciting phase of the relationship is the "infatuation stage." This newly discovered friend is a mystery to us. She is alluring. He is exciting. We are intrigued by the possibilities, excited about what we are yet to discover. There is a fascinating newness about the relationship. Our curiosity is piqued! (Caution: Do not confuse this intense feeling with love.)

This "curiosity factor" creates a huge amount of passion and momentum early in the relationship and drives us to want to spend more time together, to get to know each other better. It creates the desire to take the relationship to the next level.

But, what happens when the newness wears off and our curiosity is satisfied? "Oh, I guess you aren't as fascinating as I thought." How long does it take for a person to become familiar, or for us to take him or her for granted? How long before his or her cute quirks become annoying habits?

A relationship that never grows beyond the infatuation stage, or becomes physical too soon (caution: sexual activity before marriage tends to stunt relational growth), will generally last no more than six to twelve months. It must either grow or end.

Infatuation is not an end goal; it is an incentive to grow. It is the "love is blind" phase of an intimate relationship. Even an introverted computer geek can market himself effectively during the infatuation period.

A lot of marriages never survive the "honeymoon stage." Those first two or three years can be a real thrill ride. Or they can be torture, as the newness begins to slowly wear off and the daily grind of going to school, living life, and paying bills sets in.

This is where we begin to see issues with "truth in advertising." Jack's veneer cracks and he reveals himself as an abusive control freak, or Jill starts drinking heavily. A lot of marriages are annulled because they did not know each other long enough to get below the surface and discover where the defects are.

Much of the struggle in the early years of a marriage is trying to restore that lost intensity and passion we had for each other when we were dating. What happened to the curiosity? What happened to the mystery? Now my partner is just puzzling! Have I already learned all the interesting stuff about my partner? Now what?

The challenge is to create new "newness."

Create some new excitement and wonder. There are mysteries and surprises yet to be explored. Your marriage can be wonder-full. Fill it with newness (see MM #13).

Date your spouse. (I do not mean Carbon-14 dating. He or she is not that old.) Go on regular dates to new places. See new things. Go on new adventures. Do the little things you did before that made your partner fall in love with you in the first place.

Create anticipation and excitement. You invested a lot of time, energy, and money into the relationship early on. Why did you stop? We have already talked about how a little chaos and unpredictability can keep a relationship interesting. Make sure you and your partner have something exciting to look forward to. Keep your marriage fresh and alive.

Cast a vision for the future. Develop a sense of purpose for your marriage. This may involve some kind of service to others. "Together" is the operative word here.

Now go out there and do something mysterious that will keep you and your spouse intrigued.

Personal prayer:
Lord, you have created a mysterious and fascinating universe. Thank you for the gift of curiosity. Help me to constantly foster newness, mystery, and a vision for the future in my marriage. May I never lose my sense of fascination and curiosity with my partner and with you.

The Grinch

I love Dr. Seuss. What an incredibly creative mind he had and what a wonderful command of words, both real and imaginary! He made "nonsense" fashionable for three generations.

From *The Cat in the Hat*[1] to *Yertle the Turtle*.[2] From *Green Eggs and Ham*[3] to *On Beyond Zebra*.[4] He told delightful stories with memorable characters and poetry. I can quote many of them to this day. One of my favorites is *How the Grinch Stole Christmas*.[5]

I am fascinated by the events that bring about either positive or negative change in the lives of people, and the Grinch is a great example.

Bullied and ridiculed as a youngster, the Grinch withdrew from society and became isolated, lonely, and bitter. His world shrank to the size of his cave and so did his heart. He could not stand to be around anyone who was happy, and the residents of Whoville were perpetually happy, especially at Christmas.

They reminded him of how miserable he was, so he decided to make them miserable, too, by stealing Christmas.

As he is carrying out this nefarious deed, Cindy Lou Who enters his life. She is an innocent wisp of a Who girl, naïve and easily fooled, in the Grinch's mind. And yet, she is the strongest person in the whole story.

So, Take-away #1 is: Never underestimate the influence of a small child speaking the truth!

The other thing that intrigues me about this story is what happens to the Grinch. His victory is short-lived when he discovers that he has not ruined Christmas at all, and that he has been looking at life from the wrong perspective.

An amazing transformation takes place as he realizes that the joy the residents of Whoville experience is not based on gifts and lights and trees, but on loving each other and sharing their lives together.

And the Grinch's heart changed. It grew "three sizes that day."

For the first time in his life the Grinch was able to experience love and joy!

If you have been burned by love, you, like the Grinch, may believe that love is a limited resource, that there is only so much to go around and someone else got in line ahead of you and stole your share. You may have come to believe that you are unworthy and do not deserve to be loved.

Well, the Grinch just proved you wrong!

When you have been hurt, what starts out as healthy self-care can easily become self-pity and self-centeredness. That is how you shrink your heart. You withdraw and say, "I will never let anyone hurt me again."

Have you ever said that?

Many years ago I was living in Santa Barbara, California, near the beach, and was going through a very difficult period of my life. I was living alone. I was depressed, and some days I could barely function. My world had imploded and become very small.

I walked down to the secluded beach near my apartment and saw a woman sitting on the beach writing in the sand with her finger. She looked very depressed. (It takes one to know one, right?)

I finally got up the courage to walk up and ask her if she needed someone to talk to. She looked up with tears streaming down her face and said that she had been praying that God would send someone to talk with.

She had written "Jesus" in the sand.

I sat down and listened to her sad story of hurt and abuse for about thirty minutes, then had to leave to go to work. I prayed for her and then left. I never knew her name or saw her again, but the most amazing thing happened to me.

I didn't walk the half mile home—I floated. My depression was gone! And it never returned.

The lesson of the Grinch and the woman at the beach (Take-away #2) is that when we step outside of ourselves and our shrunken world and begin to focus on others, our capacity to give and to receive love increases dramatically. Our hearts get bigger and we realize that love is an *infinite* resource. It never runs out!

If your marriage has become distant, cold, or loveless, the first step toward restoration is to step outside of your own hurt and focus your attention on your spouse. If you concentrate on his or her needs, concerns, and hurt, you will see your spouse's heart warm and heal.

And you may look back and realize that your own heart "grew three sizes that day."

Personal Prayer:
Lord, do not allow me the self-indulgence of withdrawing from life and retreating into my Cave of Personal Misery. Expand my heart to the size of yours and give me enough love of others to pour myself into their lives as you have done.

100% All In

Once upon a time there were three frogs sitting on a log in a pond. They all decided to jump into the water. How many frogs were left sitting on the log?

If you said, "None," you were WRONG!

The correct answer is—all of them, because *deciding* to do something is not enough. You have to *commit* to doing something and then turn that commitment into *action*.

If you go sky-diving and keep one foot firmly planted inside the plane while the other dangles in thin air, your parachute will never perform as intended. The same holds true in the swimming pool. If you are clinging for dear life to the diving board, you will never experience the thrill of diving safely into the water. You will never learn to skate by clinging to the rail, or ride a bicycle until you take off the training wheels and put your feet on the pedals.

What is it that keeps us from making the commitment and taking the leap of faith that will result in learning a new skill or conquering a new challenge?

Fear does! And it is ably assisted by its cousin, control!

We fear failing. We fear falling. We fear speaking in public. We fear spiders and snakes. But, mostly, we fear losing control. If we let go of total control, bad things might happen to us.

We hope that we can experience the same thrill of an amazing dive without having to make a commitment to actually jump off. We want to reap the benefits without having to pay the price.

But, life does not work that way.

This attitude is prevalent in relationships, as well. I have met hundreds of couples who thought they could experience the joy and satisfaction of a healthy marriage without actually having to get married! They claimed to love each other and wanted a long-term relationship, but were afraid to commit to marriage.

I believe it is because they fear divorce. I suppose they are thinking that if they do not get married, then they cannot get divorced. That seems silly to me, because the separation rate of unmarried couples is higher than the divorce rate!

In his book, *No More Christian Nice Guy,* Paul Coughlin states that there is a commonly held view in America today that says, "If I live small, my troubles will be few."[1] He asserts that this belief is absolutely **not** true! We will never experience all that marriage can be until we take the risk, pay the price, and jump in head first.

To derive all of the joy and blessings from our relationship with God and with our spouse, we must be 100% all in. No back-up plan. No outside options or backdoor exits. Nothing stashed away in case it doesn't work out. Making a contribution to your marriage is not good enough. It requires total commitment! And the blessings will follow.

Put ALL of your chips on the table!

Do you remember the story of the chicken and the pig who wanted to go out for breakfast? The chicken suggested they have ham and eggs, but the pig protested, saying, "For you that is merely a contribution, but for me it is a total commitment."

Without risk there can be no gain. Without struggle there can be no victory; and, in most cases, without taking the risk of failure there can be no success. If you want your life to be risk free with guaranteed safety and success, you are doomed to mediocrity!

But if you want more from life, your marriage, and from God, you have to take the risk.

Go ahead. Risk it all. Step off the diving board. I dare you.

Personal prayer:
Lord, "I believe. Help my unbelief" (Mark 9:24, ESV). Help me to take risks in my marriage and in my faith. Help me to step forward with eyes wide open, trusting you to provide and protect, and let go of trying to be in control of my own life. I commit myself to you and to my spouse.

No New Damage

I heard a story once about a young man who was walking down the street and passed by a house where an old man was sitting on his front porch in a rocking chair. The old man's equally old hound dog was sitting at his feet howling for all he was worth.

The guy asked the old man, "Is that your hound dog?"
"Yup," the old man replied.
"What's he howling about?"
"I suspect he's howlin' 'cause he's sittin' on a rusty nail."
The old man seemed unconcerned.
"Why don't he get up and move?"
The old man smiled slightly and said, "I guess it don't hurt that bad."

Isn't that the truth?! Sometimes we prefer to lie there in painful misery and howl about our awful lives, rather than getting up and doing something about it. We hate to change things—even if it will improve our lives and reduce our discomfort.

Positive change requires effort and motivation. *Negative* change is easy and requires little effort. (Remember the 2nd Law of Thermodynamics?)

Bad habits only require that you do nothing different, which may be why "drift" is so common (see MM #8).

Personal growth, including developing good habits, is the result of deliberate effort.

What keeps you from losing weight, getting in shape, or working on your marriage? "I guess it don't hurt that bad."

Pain is a powerful motivator to fix what is wrong in your life. When it hurts badly enough, you will try to change.

Usually the first thing you look for is a quick, easy solution. Bad news—there is no easy solution. There is no easy way to lose weight; no easy way to repair a damaged marriage.

Positive change requires motivation, determination, a strategic plan, and consistent effort.

There are two things that must be done to fix your marriage.

First, stop hurting your relationship. Healing cannot begin until you stop causing damage to it. Whatever you are doing to cause damage to your spouse and your marriage ... **Stop it! Now!**

If your anger, lying, selfishness, addictions, distractions, insensitivity, workaholism, gaming, internet activity, pornography, perfectionism, anxiety, fear, or _____ is causing harm to your marriage, STOP IT!

NO NEW DAMAGE! You cannot begin the process of rebuilding your marriage until you stop tearing it down. Quit adding to the pile of offenses.

I challenge you to go for a whole *week* without creating any new damage.

"But, you don't understand. It's not easy to stop _____." If it were easy, we would not be having this conversation. You would have already done it. The problem is either **ignorance** or **apathy**. Either you do not know what to do or you are not motivated to do it.

The cure for **ignorance** is knowledge. Keep reading this book.

The cure for **apathy** is having a "dream" that is big enough to motivate you to change. If you have a problem with motivating yourself, you need a bigger dream!

Second, whatever you did to make your spouse fall in love with you originally, do it again and again (see MM #26), and this time **don't stop**! Keep doing it until the pain is gone and you have developed good, healthy relationship habits.

If you sow good, positive seeds into your marriage, you will reap an amazing harvest.

Why did your partner fall in love with you? Not because he or she is dumber than a stick, but because you were so darn lovable!

Go be your old lovable self and get some positive energy flowing in your marriage again. Like getting in shape, it is hard at first, but the more you do it, the easier it gets.

Do it now.

Personal prayer:
Lord, implant in my heart a vision for my life and my marriage that is so captivating and exciting that it continually motivates me to change and grow. I commit to you, Lord, that I will cause no new damage to my marriage this week. Help me become an instrument of healing in my marriage.

Shedding That Excess Weight

I am currently trying to lose twenty pounds. Based on how much I love donuts, I am probably only serious about five of them. I am very disciplined about my diet. I try to eat only food.

When someone asks me how much weight I have lost, I tell them, "seventy-five pounds—the same five pounds over and over and over."

I guess I am just not very weight-conscious, unless it comes to carrying it on my back.

Years ago I did a lot of backpacking in the Sierra Nevada Mountains of California. There are few places on earth more majestic, more beautiful, and more awe-inspiring. But the wilderness can be treacherous and lethal if you are not properly prepared. We would spend weeks getting ready for our trip, buying light-weight essentials and stuffing them into little plastic bags.

We tried to anticipate every possible hazard and prepare for it. The problem was that we couldn't possibly carry everything we needed. Each additional pound on our backs equated to five additional pounds on our feet! It is amazing how many of these "essentials" got left behind to get those backpacks down to fifty or sixty pounds.

If you had that same mentality with your marriage, what a difference it would make! If you spent as much time planning and preparing for marriage as you spend planning for a camping or hunting trip, you might find yourself better equipped when adversity comes.

I have seen people carrying the most frivolous things into the back country—folding beach chairs, heavy shot guns, and BBQ grills! There are few things more disgusting than being three days into the wilderness and finding an item someone has discarded. It was too heavy and they didn't want to carry it anymore, so they just tossed it aside. Apparently, the main ascent to Mount Everest is littered with tons of trash that climbers threw away.

The same is true of marriage. If you bring unnecessary baggage into the relationship, you have to carry it. Your spouse has his or her own load to carry. Don't force your non-essentials onto your partner. You cannot afford to let your excess baggage slow you down or get in the way.

If we each have a problem and I take ownership of yours, I now have two problems and you still have one.

If that baggage is abuse, hurt or disappointment from your past, family dysfunction, unrealistic expectations, or addictions, do your best to discard it all before you embark on your journey. It is hard to enjoy a beautiful sunset if you are focused on how much your feet hurt; it's hard to have a great marriage if your past is stealing your joy.

If you need help to either "lighten your load or to strengthen your back," seek it. You and your partner will fare better for it.

1. Jesus was very clear about what we should do with our past—**give it to him and walk away from it**. Quit carrying it around! Get professional help if necessary, but do not lay it at the foot of the cross and then pick it up again.
2. **Share your burdens** with someone who can handle them. That will lighten your load.

3. **Let God create for you a future** that is overwhelmingly more exciting, amazing, and blessed than your past ever was!

If you want to have a successful marriage, talk to successful couples who have been down that trail. Learn from their mistakes and don't repeat them. Every year hikers die because they did not know the dangers or heed the warning signs. Marriages die every year for the same reasons. And don't forget to read God's Book! It is the best relationship manual ever written.

Personal prayer:
Lord, give me the clarity of vision and foresight to know what the truly essential things are in my life and my relationships. Help me to discard those which are not important. The more my eyes are clouded by these non-essentials, the more likely I am to miss the beautiful vistas along the way.

The Law of Association

The Law of Association says that you become like the people you hang around.

If you hang out with thieves, you will eventually become a thief. If you hang out with pot smokers, you will become a pot smoker, regardless of what your eighteen-year-old college freshman says!

You begin to behave like these other people. Then you begin to talk and think like them. Gradually you begin to adopt their ideas and their worldview. At that point you become one of them.

Psalm 1 describes this process of influencing someone as "walk, stand, sit." You **walk** by and are curious. You **stand** and listen, and then you **sit** and join them.

The more time you spend with others, the more you will be influenced by them.

If everyone would just spend more time with Jesus, wouldn't the world be a nicer place? Alas, I don't see that happening soon. All of our thoughts, ideas, and behaviors involve the influence of other people. Unfortunately, far too often it is a negative thing.

There is another law that I just made up—the **Law of Retinal Input**.

1. You cannot "un-see" something,
2. Everything you see, your brain remembers, and
3. You are <u>changed</u> by what you see.

You must carefully choose what you allow your eyes to see, because you *will* be impacted. You must guard your heart, your eyes, and your mind or you will become polluted by the world. Job said he made "a covenant with my eyes" (Job 31:1, NIV) not to look at things he shouldn't.

I have seen things in my life that were horrifying and are forever burned into my memory. What we see becomes a part of who we are. Ask any soldier who has seen the horror of war and death. We are forever changed by it.

The world is filled with negative influences—crime, disease, war, natural disasters, politics, immorality, strange philosophies. If you do not guard your mind and your heart from these things, you may become stained by the world.

How can you keep yourself from becoming contaminated by all the ideological pollution and negativity in your personal environment?

How would you go about cleaning up a polluted pond on your property?

The first thing you need to do is **stop making it worse**! Quit pouring more pollutants into the pond and into your brain (see MM #29)! Don't let any of that toxic mess get onto you or into you.

You must jealously guard your eyes, ears, and mind from negative influences—TV shows, music, books, websites, or people. Do not let bad choices become bad habits. Take your scissors and "snip" them out of your life!

The second thing you should do is to **flood your pond (mind) with fresh, clean water (wholesome thoughts)**. Give your mind a chance to heal and to revive. You need to inundate your life with positive inputs—wholesome books, movies, music, activities, and relationships. Surround yourself and your family with people and experiences that will lift you up and encourage you to become a better person.

Then, **practice sanctification**. That means, walk down a different street. Hang out with different people. Experience renewal. It may take time to become the new person God wants you to be. Be patient with yourself and others. Sanctification is a process that requires a lifetime.

If your marriage has become polluted, the same process applies. Healing takes time.

Fill your eyes with the beauty God has made. Fill your mind with his word and your heart with praise.

Do not break these two laws, the **Law of Association** and the **Law of Retinal Input.** Instead, YOU become the one who is influencing others for good and not for evil.

You can be the positive force that changes others!

Personal prayer:
Lord, help me to choose my associates wisely. Protect my eyes from seeing things they should not and my ears from attending to any malicious speech. Keep me from places I should not go. Most of all, help me to become the "light" that influences other people to do good.

Don't Be Surprised

I don't like surprises! Pleasant little surprises are okay, like driving to Downtown Anywhere, USA, and not encountering much traffic, or rounding a bend in the road and seeing the most beautiful sunset, or getting something better than I expected for my birthday.

There are special surprises that only happen a few times in your life, like "Surprise, honey, I'm pregnant!" Those are all okay, but many surprises are startling, unexpected (by definition), and can be life-altering in a negative way.

Surprises are unpredictable.

If you have a problem with attention-deficit, hyperactivity, or are an adrenaline junkie, then chaos may be exciting to you. But if you tend more towards the obsessive-compulsive, control freak end of the spectrum, then surprises are disruptive, chaotic, unexpected, and unmanageable.

I don't like *big* surprises. They mess up my routine.

A good, healthy marriage should be filled with lots of *little* surprises:

- a love note surreptitiously stuffed into your lunch bag,
- a chocolate kiss anytime, anywhere,
- unexpected time together—alone!

These unanticipated, delightful experiences add spice to your marriage and keep your spouse interested and engaged—a *manageable* amount of the unexpected.

Life may be full of little surprises, but don't fill it with **shocking revelations!**

I enjoyed the movie "True Lies"[1] with Arnold Schwarzenegger and Jamie Lee Curtis. She is shocked to find out that her boring but dutiful insurance executive husband is, in real life, a government spy. Most of the story is about their humorous attempts to beat the bad guys. In typical Hollywood fashion they eventually succeed, but the process is dangerous, frightening, and very exciting. In the real world, this kind of revelation would permanently damage or destroy the marriage.

Whether it is subtle verbal abuse that suddenly becomes physical, or the discovery of an addiction or infidelity, your partner reveals a part of his or her character that you were never aware of before.

Spouses are commonly shocked and paralyzed by this kind of revelation. They go into denial, feel guilty, blame themselves, or beat themselves up for being "so stupid and blind."

But, what couples usually do *not* do is take the *right* kind of action. Talking to their drinking buddies or friends at work will not help. They need to get professional help and deal with it immediately!

If you are dating or engaged to be married, take your time and get to know this person well. That usually takes twelve to eighteen months. An old maxim says that the "best predictor of future behavior is past behavior."

Look for warning signs and do not ignore them. If you are married and are struggling with little indiscretions, get help, now!

Now, go out there and delight your spouse this week with the right kind of surprise.

Personal prayer:
Lord, thank you for the surprises you place in my path, even the unsettling ones, because surprises stir up my wonder and curiosity and shake me out of my doldrums and stodginess. Give me the curiosity to seek the surprises you have in store for me today, especially that wonderfully surprising spouse I share my life with.

Sherlock Holmes

"Elementary, my dear Watson."

Since the time these words first appeared in print, Sherlock Holmes[1] has fascinated people with his powers of deduction.

Sir Arthur Conan Doyle created a character who was a master at paying attention to detail. The master sleuth had a knack for being able to attach significance to the smallest clues at a crime scene and to reconstruct an accurate account of what transpired.

I love to watch television and movie versions, whether the actor is Robert Downey, Jr., Jeremy Brett, Benedict Cumberbatch, or Jonny Lee Miller.

I am fascinated by Holmes's breadth of knowledge and astounded by his complete ineptitude in relationships. It is a good thing he never got married! However, if he had, he would have recognized that "*little* things are symbolic of *big* things."

One of the biggest issues in working with married couples is the husband's complaint that his wife attaches too much significance to insignificant things—that she makes big deals out of little things.

But, according to Sherlock Holmes, there are no insignificant or meaningless things—there are only clues. I agree with this 100%. If you understand the message of the clue, you will understand what has just happened, what is really going on.

Authorities as diverse as Mark Gungor (*Laugh Your Way to a Better Marriage*, 2007)[2] and Barbara DeAngelis (*What Women Want Men to Know*, 2001)[3] have stated that women are all about relationships. They define themselves by their relationships ("I am _____'s daughter, mother, sister, friend," etc.). They derive their sense of well-being and self-esteem from the quality and healthiness of their relationships.

Ladies, don't get mad at me if this does not describe you. It is what most people would consider "normal" for most women.

Because of this amazing innate characteristic, girls tend to be more socially adept than boys. They are more attuned to the nuances of relationships. They communicate more emotionally, relationally, and frequently than boys, and they are more aware of fluctuations (temperature changes) in their closest relationships. Remember, all communication is a commentary on the status of the relationship (see MM #12).

Guys, if you want to improve your chances of understanding what your wife is REALLY saying, then assume that 95% of the time (at least) it will have something to do with the current status of your relationship.

You think I'm exaggerating? Not this time, Bubba. Everything you say and do, or forget to say or do, will be interpreted in the context of, "What does this tell me about how he feels about me?"

If you can accept this, the lights will come on, and her responses that have confused you in the past will suddenly become clear.

If women are a mystery, and your wife is particularly mysterious, then you need to put on your Deerstalker hat and grab your Meerschaum pipe and begin examining the clues. They may be subtle, obscure, clever, sneaky, or hidden, but they are not insignificant!

Deciphering the clues may help you unlock the mystery that is your wife and open up whole new vistas of understanding.

"It's elementary, my dear Watson."

Personal prayer:
Lord, help me to perceive the meaning behind the words my wife is using. Help me to understand what she is saying about us and to pick up the little clues that will help me to love her like she needs to be loved.

Umpires—Defining Reality

When my boys were young, we participated in the obligatory soccer and baseball seasons, every fall and spring for twelve years.

Because I had some experience in sports officiating, I occasionally was called on to stand behind home plate and umpire baseball games. I liked the job. It changed my perspective on the game and gave me a greater understanding of and respect for the people who do it professionally.

Umpiring relates to one of the biggest stressors that couples face in their marriages—parenting. There is a constant stream of little things that we disagree over when it comes to how we raise our children, and it can create inordinate amounts of stress.

I have seen marriages crumble because the couple could not agree on parenting styles.

Parenting is definitely *not* for the faint of heart, nor is it an exact science. (Have you heard that insanity is genetic? You get it from your children.)

Children do not come with their own personal instruction manual. They easily master the art of shredding your resolve, your good intentions, your will, and your sanity. It is critical that you protect your marriage from these selfish and demanding home invaders.

The problem comes down to who defines reality in your home?

Many people do not understand what the role of an umpire is. It is **to define what just happened and make a judgment based on the rules of the game.** It is also the goal of the umpire to interfere in the game as little as possible, but as often as necessary.

If there were no rules, there would be no need for officiating. (Pay attention here, parents.) <u>Your home must have rules and someone to enforce them</u>. That same someone must make judgments when a violation has occurred and mete out appropriate consequences. Only two people qualify for that honor—the parents.

I occasionally encountered players, coaches and even parents on the sidelines who saw things a certain way and believed they knew what reality was. They were wrong!

I had to remind them that the play is not *anything* until I define it, and then, that *is* what it is; my definition *is* reality, regardless of what you thought you might have seen." You thought your runner was safe, but I defined him as out, therefore, he is out.

Did I ever make a wrong call?	No. Once made, each call became right, by definition.
Did I ever make a bad call?	That depended on which team they supported.
Did they ever question a call?	Rarely. I will explain why in the next Marriage Minute.

As parents, you sometimes have to make difficult or unpopular judgment calls. Effective parenting has never been very popular among its constituency. You must be un-swayed by your declining popularity in the parenting polls.

Regardless of what your children may want reality to be, it is up to *you* to define it for them.

Children do not begin life "self-defined." They have no idea what their physical, mental, and emotional limitations are. It is up to you, as parents, to help them discover *safely* what their limitations are, and who they will eventually become.

As much as your son might like to fly like a bird, putting on his Superman pajamas will not make it happen. But someone needs to tell him that, or he might give it a try. I have a T-shirt that jokingly reads, "I would be unstoppable except for law enforcement and physics." A young boy is not an expert in either of those.

The whole point of parenting is to help our children make it to adulthood knowing

- who they are,
- what the realities and limitations of the world are, and
- what the rules are for living in this society.

They need to be able to determine for themselves when they have hit a fair ball or if it went foul.

They also need to come to terms with the fact that sometimes other people get to define reality for them, whether they agree to it or not.

I recently got a speeding ticket. I was not driving dangerously and was not aware that the speed limit had suddenly changed, but the local law enforcement officer defined me as driving 25 mph over the limit.

I didn't like it, but I wisely accepted his definition. By the way, there was a $250 consequence that came with it. Sometimes, reality is painful.

So, Moms and Dads, you are the definers of reality, the umpires in your home. For the sake of your children and your marriage, define reality well.

Next time, we will look at "Ten Rules for Calling a Good Game."

Personal prayer:
Lord, only you can ultimately define me because you created and sustain me. But, as a parent, you have given me the responsibility of helping my children discover who they are and how to operate in a complex and difficult world. Give me wisdom each day to make a correct call. There is a life at stake here.

Umpires
Making and Enforcing the Call

There are **Ten Rules for Calling a Good Game** practiced by umpires; I believe these rules will help us with our parenting and keep our marriages healthy and strong.

But first, a warning and a definition.

WARNING: If your primary motivation is for your children to *like* you, then you are in deep trouble.

They will love you, but they will not always *like* you or your decisions. Not required. Get over it.

DEFINITION: "Parent in Charge" This is the adult who was first on the scene or was present when "it" happened. That adult will define the event and make the decision. The other adult is there for back up and support only. Nod in agreement, but keep your mouth shut. Do not interfere.

1. **Know the rules.** Three strikes and you are out. *Every* time. Never two, never four.

   Both parents must agree on the rules of the home and apply them consistently. The purpose for rules in the first place is not for your own comfort and convenience, but to provide structure and discipline for those who have not matured enough to make good decisions on their own.

2. **You define reality.** Your children may not like it and will test it, but reality is whatever you decide it is. Never apologize for enforcing a house rule. After all, it is *your* house, *your* rules.

   It is important that the family rules make sense, are not archaic, obsolete, unnecessary, or totally arbitrary. If your child is five years or older, "Because I said so!" is not a legitimate response.

   If you don't have a good reason for a house rule, get rid of it. Remember the Apostle Paul's admonition to fathers, "Do not exasperate your children" (Ephesians 6:4, NIV).

3. **No double standards allowed.** Unless there is an age or maturity exemption, *all* rules apply to *everyone*, even the adults. If teenagers must say where they are going and when they will be back, so must the adults.

4. **Be clear on your role.** As the umpire, I called balls and strikes and covered home plate and third base. The other official covered the outfield and first and second base.

   Don't "make a call" from the other side of the house. You are neither omniscient nor omnipresent.

5. **Make a call that everyone can hear clearly and understand.** When I was umpiring games, there was no doubt what the call was. ("Clear" and "loud" are not the same thing.)

   Be direct and confident. If it is to their advantage, your children will deliberately misinterpret the message. Screaming does not improve understanding, nor does it guarantee compliance.

6. **If you are unsure of the correct call, consult.** Football referees often consult with each other or watch the replay to be sure they have made an accurate call. The players, coaches, and fans must wait for a decision.

   If the other parent has a better perspective on the circumstances, defer to his or her judgment. Take the time to consult with each other before making a decision. Ninety percent of parenting decisions can wait ten to fifteen minutes while you talk it over. Talk it over until you come to an agreement you can *both* support. Then, when you make your decision, no waffling or changing your mind! This is where you strengthen your marriage.

7. **Never lose emotional control.** Do not attempt to make a parenting decision when you are tired, upset, hungry, or angry. Re-read Stupidville (MM #19) and Time Out (MM #20). You can be loud, but you must remain positive.

   Never blame the child for your loss of emotional control. He or she might have done something you don't like, but it is *your* choice to be calm or to fly into a rage.

8. **Never overturn the other official's call.** If your partner makes a unilateral decision, you do not have to agree with it, but you do have to support it. You can discuss it privately later when you debrief the experience together. Seriously, is it worth hurting your relationship because your partner gave your child a cookie?

   Most issues are not that big. Keep things in perspective.

9. **Do not play favorites.** Be fair and impartial. No one ever doubted my impartiality when I umpired a game because I had no investment in which team prevailed.

    The single biggest complaint of spouses with blended families is, "You treat *your* kids better than you treat *mine!*" You are responsible for the physical and emotional welfare of *every* member of the family.

10. **Make a quality call and be confident that you have done so.** The best umpires are the best trained and have the most confidence. This was the reason why my umpiring calls were rarely questioned. I was well-trained and confident in my ability to make good calls.

    The best parents seek help from others until they become experienced professionals.

Unlike baseball, family rules *do* change over time. As kids get older, take on more responsibility, and become more independent, day-to-day reality begins to change and so do the rules.

There are some rules that will never change because they reflect the values and morals of the family as a whole. "No, your boyfriend may not spend the night here (nor you there), ever!"

In a world full of healthy, mature people there would be no need for rules. But that is not the world we live in, and is why we need referees, umpires, police, and judges.

You have eighteen years to prepare your children to survive in a competitive adult world. One of the best ways to do that is to establish and enforce balanced, fair, flexible, and appropriate rules.

Now go out there and call a good game.

Personal prayer:
Lord, help me to be balanced in my parenting and to trust my partner's instincts, as well. May I never exasperate my children with selfish or petty rules, but consistently enforce the important ones. Give me the wisdom and maturity to know what each member of my family needs to become more like Christ.

Balance is Overrated

Unless you are The Flying Wallendas or a Chinese acrobatic group, balance is overrated.

There are times in which balance is absolutely necessary—riding a bicycle, ice skating, tightrope-walking. Losing balance at these times can be particularly painful.

I was brought up, just like you, to believe that we should be balanced in all areas of our lives. I can agree that having your checking account balanced at the end of the month is a good idea, but other kinds of balance are less motivating for me.

Being out of balance is so much easier! As long as I have overdraft protection, the bank doesn't mind, right? Why fret over a few pennies (or a few hundred dollars, for that matter)?

I admit that eating a nutritionally balanced lunch is healthier than having a chocolate bar, three doughnuts, and a bag of tortilla chips (but not nearly as emotionally satisfying). But putting together a healthy meal to take to work requires time, effort, self-discipline, and forethought. Blech!

A pendulum that is *not* swinging from one extreme to the other is not very interesting. A see-saw (or teeter-totter, depending on where you grew up) demonstrates that imbalance is more fun. A balanced teeter-totter is only fun for a few seconds. How many times were you left hanging in the air because your teeter-totter opponent outweighed you by thirty pounds?

Married life is very demanding (surprise). We spend a lot of time trying to balance career, jobs, parenting, social commitments, chores, church, exercise, sleep, football, hunting, etc. We become stressed, overwhelmed, predictable, and boring!

It is no surprise that after a few years of this, our marriages can lose some spark.

Sometimes you just *have* to go to an extreme! No one ever got famous for being average. Average, routine, dull, mundane marriages are ... BORING! (Oops, did I say that out loud?)

So, how do you re-ignite the fire? How do you keep yourself and your mate interested and excited about your future together? GET EXTREME!

Dream big! *Extremely* big! It doesn't matter how old you are or how long you have been married. You need dreams, aspirations and a future to strive towards.

Love to *extremes*. Laugh loudly and often. *Extremely* often.

Be an extremist! Be *extremely* positive, encouraging, caring, playful, passionate, sacrificial, patient, generous, kind (and all that other stuff that the Apostle Paul talks about in 1 Corinthians 13).

Discover your partner's top five or six most important needs and meet them *extremely well*. Don't just fill the cup, make it overflow, always!

Ladies, if you are not making yourself and your marriage exciting and doing things to keep your husband engaged, motivated, and attentive, he may get bored and spend more time at work than with you. You have to be more interesting, exciting, and engaging than his work! How hard could *that* be?

Gentlemen, if you do not keep pursuing your wife and keep her excited about you and your relationship ... if you do not keep stoking her dreams about the future and showing her how amazing it is to be married to you, she may wander off and spend more time with her girlfriends than with you. You have to be more interesting than her girlfriends! For most of us guys, that is not going to be an easy task.

Sometimes we just have to go to such an extreme in our marriage that we throw everything else temporarily out of balance! Take some risks. Be silly with each other. Throw caution to the wind. Do the unexpected.

Now go and love your spouse ... *extremely well.*

Personal prayer:
Lord, you have gone to great extremes to redeem me because of your great love for me. You made an extreme sacrifice of love to save me from eternal death. Fill me with your great love so that I can love my spouse extremely well.

Pepé Le Pew

I scored major points on Valentine's Day this year. My record is not very good when it comes to picking outstanding Valentine's Day gifts, so it was nice to do something right that made my wife's eyes light up. I got her a plush Pepé Le Pew[1] that says something romantic when you press his foot.

"I pick you. I pick you again. Lucky me ... I pick you *every* time." That's her favorite.

I like Pepé Le Pew. Not just because of his French accent and suave demeanor, but because of his indomitable spirit and his belief that love will overcome any obstacle or deficiency.

Since he is a skunk, his deficiencies are obvious and plentiful.

The focus of his amorous attention is always a black she-kitty that has accidentally obtained a white stripe and is mistaken by Pepé for another skunk. As she desperately attempts to escape his "overwhelming presence," he is patient and undeterred. He refuses to accept rejection.

I don't remember if he ever actually got the girl in the end, but he never gave up trying. His eyes were fixed on his heart's desire and he knew that his persistence would be rewarded.

Isn't this how God is with us? He keeps chasing us until we finally give up and accept his love. He is relentless. Frances Thompson, an

English poet of the late 19th century, referred to God as the "Hound of Heaven."[2]

Nothing will stop God in fulfilling his desire to express his love for us.

Guys (or Ladies), if you are going through a particularly difficult time in your marriage, try being a little like Pepé Le Pew.

"How do I do that?" you wonder. I'm glad you asked.

1. Focus *all* of your attention on the object of your desire *all* of the time. How do you think you overcame his or her objections in the first place? Having a burning desire for someone can become very attractive.
2. Do not get discouraged, no matter how much he or she runs the other way. The object of your desire *may* be testing you to see how serious you really are (see MM #38 and #39).
3. Be patient, determined, relentless, gentle, loving, and respectful.
4. Never give up. Never, never, never, never. (This is NOT permission to be a stalker. Pursuit is not the same as stalking. Being creepy is not very lovable.)
5. Do not just give your partner his or her heart's desire. *Be* her heart's desire. *Be* his heart's desire.
6. It never hurts to steal some romantic phrases from experts like Pepé Le Pew. Someone else's eloquence will work for you, if you are sincere.
7. Do NOT smell like a skunk! Do not come on too strong or cross the line into becoming abusive. The goal is not to overwhelm or to coerce, but to persuade with love.

I have seen many couples give up in discouragement when their repeated attempts to connect with each other have been frustrated or ineffective. Whether your partner is rejecting your pursuit and creating distance in the relationship, or you are trying to reduce the effects of normal drift, that is precisely when you need to intensify your resolve to never give up.

Even if you "stink" at pursuing your spouse, remember what Pepé had to overcome.

Love is the most powerful force in the universe. It is an irresistible force. It is even stronger than fear. Persistent love can abolish all fear, for it is fear that causes us to run away from love (see 1 John 4:18).

Husbands and wives, you really only have one task, and there is only one secret to a successful and fulfilling marriage—win your partner's heart back today!

Now, go out there and be a relentlessly romantic pursuer.

Personal prayer:
Lord, give me the eyes to see what my wife's (husband's) heart's desire is, and the persistence to never give up pursuing her (him) all the days of our marriage. I may sometimes stink, but I desire to pursue her (him) as relentlessly as you have pursued me.

The Cloak of Invisibility

My wife has a super power! Sure, sure, I know, every woman has the incredible super power of reading minds, and moms can certainly see through walls; but that's not what I'm talking about. I'm talking about a real, honest-to-goodness superpower.

My wife has the ability to become completely invisible!

I first discovered this power early in our marriage. We would go to the grocery store; I would turn aside briefly, and when I turned back, she had completely vanished. Disappeared! There were times when I was looking directly at her and could not see her at all. Amazing, right?

Right now you are probably saying, "That's nothing! I can look my son directly in the eyes and tell him to pick up his dirty laundry and he will neither see nor hear me."

Yes, but that has more to do with motivation than superpowers. I was actually *trying* to see her. I would wander around the entire store two or three times looking for her and finally find her not more than ten feet away from where we had been.

One of us had gotten lost!

After a few years of this I began to realize that she had not really disappeared, nor put on her Cloak of Invisibility, but was playing Hide and Seek. She was sneaking around the store hiding behind end caps, deliberately avoiding me.

She might tell you a different story, but this is how I remember it. And, you know, I never exaggerate!

Nowadays, if she disappears in the grocery store, I just go up to the manager and ask if the store's "Wife Locator App" is currently activated. Usually they look at me strangely or laugh at me, but offer no helpful solutions. (Thank the Lord for cell phones.)

I confess that it took way too long for me to figure out that she was not really trying to ditch me, but was hiding and watching me trying to find her. (In the meantime I got a lot of exercise.)

What took even longer to figure out was *why* she was doing it.

She wanted to see me make the effort to find her. She wanted to be pursued! (Someone flip on the light switch and say, "Bingo.")

It seems that there is a direct correlation between how much I love her, want her, value her, and how much effort and desire I put into pursuing her. This is the stuff of every romantic comedy, Disney animated feature, westerns, and almost every Broadway musical.

After thirty years of marriage she will occasionally test me to see if I am still interested. I usually pass the test now, but I didn't always.

Perhaps you are like a lot of men who tend to be very literal in their communication and tend to think that when she says, "Go away" or "Leave me alone" she means, "Go away and leave me alone." Strangely enough, that *may* not be what she is really saying.

Sometimes she may mean, "I don't feel good about myself or our relationship right now. Come pursue me and tell me how important I am to you."

Do not let your fear of rejection get in the way of pursuing her. (**Important note:** There are some women who prefer to be mostly left alone. For her, pursuit will require a different tactic. But even she probably does not want you to go very far away and still wants you to be thinking about her constantly.)

Remember Snow White[1] and Sleeping Beauty[2]? Boy falls in love. Boy loses girl. **Boy overcomes great obstacles to get girl back.** They live happily ever after!

This is the answer, guys.

I don't know what your wife's superpower is, but what I do know is you must **never** stop pursuing her, even after she lets you catch her.

Personal Prayer:
Lord, give me the fire in my heart to never stop pursuing my wife. Give me the wisdom to discern when she is running away to see if I am still interested enough to pursue her, or if she just wants to be left alone for a while (which, so far, has been never).

The Chick Flick

This is Gina. Jerry and I decided it was time for a woman's perspective in the *Marriage Minutes*.

Let me begin by admitting up front that I like to be pursued.

There, I said it. I admit it, though it is humbling for me to do so.

Judging by the success of the romance movie genre, there are a lot of other women out there who like to be pursued as well.

There is a formula to these "chick flicks" which makes women love them. It goes something like this:

- Man and Woman meet and there is an instant attraction.
- Both of them try to hide it and remain shy acquaintances, but the attraction is real.
- The relationship grows. They have daily spats, fabulous adventures, and stylish wardrobes.
- Something happens to separate the two—a giant misunderstanding, an accident, a job in a distant city, or one being captured by a pirate.
- Approximately one day to a week passes with both feeling okay about the separation (especially the man), unless it was a kidnapping.
- Man suddenly realizes that he can't live without Woman.
- Man goes to great lengths, sparing no expense, with great danger to life and limb, to rescue her or reunite with her.

- He finds her, rescues her, and vanquishes her captor—all without messing up her hair or makeup.
- Woman acts surprised but pleased.
- She realizes that she has always loved him.
- They live happily ever after.

The writers of these movies have tapped into something deep within women. In the heart of every woman is the secret desire to be pursued and found. I say "secret" because some women might not realize this fact, and men certainly don't. ("Amen," says Jerry.)

Contrary to political correctness (I'll just have to say it), God put in women a need to feel lovely and to be the object of a man's desire. He put in men a complementary need to conquer something and rescue someone. Yes, God made us this way! (Read *Wild at Heart*[1] by John Eldredge for a fuller expression of this view.)

Tragically, past abuse or faulty teaching might have completely suppressed these natural desires in both men and women.

But this is the reason that women sometimes play hard to get (before marriage) and then later inflict their husbands with the silent treatment. In both cases we are NOT wanting our men to leave us alone for very long! (Oh, this is so hard to admit.)

In today's world women are being taught that we should not be vulnerable and should not play games. (When it is part of our souls, is it still considered a game?)

This is also the reason that little boys love to play with toy guns and swords, build forts, and maybe even rescue a fair damsel in distress (if there happens to be a little girl nearby who is willing to play along).

Young men now are being taught that *it is not right* to pursue or protect women, that we don't need it and that we DON'T WANT the very desires that God instilled in us. But we *really do* want them!

Plus, many movies (including these chick flicks) and TV shows make men look clueless and weak, or like bumbling fools. This is why men don't like chick flicks. Why pay good money to go watch men get belittled and humiliated? They would rather go to an action hero movie, where they can feel virile, conquer something, and rescue someone. They want to be heroes!

Women, make your husband feel like a brave warrior, a hero! Tell him how much you appreciate the things he does to support and protect the family. Admire and respect him.

Men, make your wife feel beautiful and deeply wanted. Sure, you will meet resistance at first because it is new and feels unreal. But, keep it up and you'll find out that you have patched an aching hole in your spouse's heart. Get out there and be a hero!

Personal prayer:
(Men) Lord, more than anything else, I want to continue to pursue my wife every day of my life as you have pursued me. I desire to be a hero in her life.

(Women) Lord, help me to lift up and encourage my husband daily in little ways and big ways to be the hero and mighty warrior you have created him to be.

Ten Commandments for Couples

Every psychologist and marriage counselor has one. Every coach, pastor, mentor, teacher, and grandma has one. We can't help it.

We *must* have a list of rules, and I am no exception.

So far in these marriage minutes I have made a lot of suggestions, challenges, and recommendations, but have not made a list of the Ten Commandments for marriage.

It is time to fix that oversight. (**Disclaimer**: I am not trying to tell you what to do. I am just describing what a healthy marriage is *not* like.)

Some years ago my father, Glover Shipp, wrote a book called *Ten Commandments for Couples*.[1] I thought it might be useful to borrow wisdom from someone who has been married 67 years to the same woman.

Each one of these rules represents an absolute truth about marriage and, if adhered to, will promote a healthy, vibrant marriage. In stark contrast, the prohibited behavior is destructive of marriage. (I don't recommend disagreeing with any of these until you have been married more than 60 years.) Among my parents and their five children there are 240 years of successful marriage as of 2015, and counting. Somebody has done something right!

So, here we go:

I.   **There is only one God** and you ain't him, and neither is your spouse. God comes first, always. Your spouse is second. Everything else, including the kids, is a distant third. No other vertical alignment will work.

II.   **Thou shalt not mess up thy priorities.** If you would sacrifice your marriage for *anything else* in the entire world, that thing is a form of idolatry. Keep your priorities straight.

III. **Thou shalt not dishonor or besmirch the name of thy spouse in public or private.** Translation: No negative talk or verbal abuse to or about your partner. Criticism is not particularly edifying either. Whatever it is, if it is not positive, don't say it!

IV.   **Remember his/her "special" days to keep them unspoiled.** Do not allow any special day, such as a birthday or an anniversary that has wonderful memories attached to it, become spoiled by a hurtful experience. You could ruin it forever.

V.   **Respect each other, thy parents, and in-laws.** Everything you say and do should be done respectfully—always! Do not lose sight of your purpose here. Is it to build up others or to tear them down? "Rejoice with those who rejoice and weep with those who weep" (Romans 12:15, NASB). You bring honor to people when you accept them as they are, where they are, and help them get to where they want to be.

VI.   **Thou shalt not kill thy marriage.** There are a million ways to kill a marriage, discouragement being one of the biggest. There is no greater love than to lay down your life for your mate (John 15:13). Do not kill your marriage. Be willing to sacrifice your life for it, instead.

VII. **Do not stray with thine eyes, thy thoughts, or thy body** (Matthew 5:27-30). Do not pick forbidden fruit. King Solomon said to "drink water from your own cistern" (Proverbs 5:15, NASB). The most intimate of all relationships is not to be shared with others.

VIII. **Thou shalt not steal from thy mate.** His or her money is yours already. That's not the issue. How about time, protection, dignity, self-worth? **Do not withhold from your mate** what he or she needs—physically, sexually, relationally, emotionally, materially. That is the same as stealing.

IX. **Thou shalt not lie to or deceive thy mate.** Do not lie *about* your mate, either. Lies and deceptions force your mate, without his or her knowledge or consent, to deal with a belief about your relationship that has nothing to do with reality. You cannot make quality relationship decisions if you do not know what reality is.

X. **Thou shalt not lust after or envy thy neighbor for his or her spouse, relationship, or anything else.** If someone has a relationship you admire, go create it in your own marriage. Let them be envious of *your* marriage.

There are consequences for breaking the rules! Healthy couples no longer have to struggle in these areas. They have overcome these struggles and moved on to more important things, such as getting down to the business of loving each other. (See the section on Major League Marriage.)

Personal prayer:
Lord, lead me not along paths that may cause me to be distracted from you or from my marriage. Strengthen my resolve to avoid temptation and engage only in pure thoughts, gracious speech, and blameless actions that edify my spouse.

Ten Rules for Wives

In case you haven't noticed lately, men and women are different!

They have different needs and different ways of doing things. They communicate and see the world differently. So it should come as no surprise to anyone that there is a different set of rules for each gender. If you want to connect with your spouse in any meaningful way, you need to abide by the "Rules of Engagement" for your gender.

For the next two Marriage Minutes we will take a look at the "Ten Rules for Wives" and "Ten Rules for Husbands" as adapted from Glover Shipp's book *Ten Commandments for Couples.*[1]

These ten are somewhat arbitrary, as there are undoubtedly dozens more we could have chosen; but these are practical and down-to-earth truths that we need to practice every day.

1. **Do not defile thy body with excessive amounts of food or alcohol,** and never use tobacco, drugs, or any other addictive substance. Any addiction is a form of idolatry. When we expect a substance to meet a need it was never intended to meet, that is idolatry. For example, food is not an appropriate substitute for love.
2. **Put thy husband first** (after God, of course). That means *before* your mother, father, children, siblings, or girlfriends and, especially, before any other man past, present, or future.
3. **Thou shalt not nag.** Nagging does not become you. Remember what Solomon said about living with a contentious woman. "Better to live on a corner of the roof

than share a house with a quarrelsome wife" (Proverbs 21:9, NIV). And, "A quarrelsome wife is like the constant dripping of a leaky roof" (Proverbs 21:15, NIV).

If you want your husband to do something, ask him. If he agrees to do it and then does not, hire it done or do it yourself. Your constant reminders will NOT make him want to cooperate or make him move any faster.

4. **Thou shalt not disrespect thy husband in public or private.** If you want him to *love you unconditionally* when you are not being very lovable, then you must *respect him unconditionally* when he is not being very respectable. (See *Love & Respect* by Dr. Emerson Eggerichs.[2])

5. **Permit no one to speak negatively about thy marriage.** Allow no one to undermine it by word or deed, or to encourage you to leave or divorce your husband. *NO ONE*!

6. **Thou shalt not withhold affection from thy husband.** You are the only legitimate source of comforting words and soothing touch he has. Do not deprive him of it (read 1 Corinthians 7:5).

7. **Thou shalt not dress provocatively in public.** Do not dress sexier for your boss, friends, or colleagues than you do for your husband. If you've got it, flaunt it in private—*only* to the *one man* who has committed his life to you and your welfare.

8. **Seek praise and adoration only from thy husband.** It is worth far more than the flattery of strangers. Earn recognition at work for your *performance*, not your *appearance*.

9. **Thou shalt maintain thy responsibilities to home, hearth, and family.** A harmonious, comfortable home is a joy in your later years. Irresponsibility that you sow in your 20s and 30s will reap a lot of drama in your 50s and beyond.

10. **Honor the Lord thy God all the days of thy life** and your children will rise up and call you blessed (Proverbs 31:28), and you will be a blessing to many others.

Ladies, if you take care of these, most of the rest of your life will take care of itself. Now, go be the wife God intended you to be.

Personal prayer:
Lord, help me to be the wife, mother, and friend that my husband and children need for me to be. May I truly grow into the image you designed for me so that I may glorify your name in all my ways.

Ten Rules for Husbands

Okay, husbands, it's your turn. We have been looking at some rules that are necessary to have a successful marriage and prevent disaster (adapted from my father's book, *Ten Commandments for Couples*[1]).

If women determine the emotional climate of a family (and I believe they do), a man's vision and leadership will determine the destiny of a family. He gives it direction, purpose, and meaning.

His Number One priority is God, and his Number One purpose is to serve God *and* love and protect his wife and children. His role is to lead by serving and guiding. All of these rules and prohibitions flow out of that lofty purpose.

1. **Do not defile thy body with tobacco, excessive amounts of alcohol, drugs, or too much junk food.** Do not indulge yourself in addictions of any kind or engage in reckless or irresponsible behavior. Addictions are a form of idolatry and slavery (see John 8:34, Romans 6 & 7).
2. **Thou shalt love, honor, protect, and defend thy wife and children at the risk of thine own life.** Make your wife the queen of your home. No one else is entitled to that honor.
3. **Thou shalt not swear at, insult, put down, yell at, or otherwise abuse thy wife in any way.** You may not call her by any name other than the one given to her by her parents or the one she legally adopted when she married you. All other "terms of endearment" must be *positive* and agreed upon by her. This *is* a big hairy deal, so handle it.

4. **Permit no one (male or female) to undermine thy marriage**, slander your wife's good name, or tell you that you should leave or divorce her. That includes family, friends, colleagues, corporations, or governments.

5. **Do not withhold love or affection from thy wife.** Be kind and gentle to her. She is the daughter of a king; treat her like one.

6. **Thou shalt not shower and shave <u>only</u> on work days.** You already "married up," Tarzan, so don't give her cause to accuse you of false advertising. Clean yourself up for your wife, not just for your boss. By the way, your abs, pecs, and glutes could use a little tightening up, too.

7. **Thou shalt not give thy wife "the Silent Treatment."** Let her into your head and your heart. Let her know that she is safe in your arms. Being unwilling to communicate is the same as being unwilling to love. It is refusing to give her the life-giving sustenance she needs to thrive.

8. **Thou shalt not keep score of slights and offenses.** Extend grace and forgiveness as freely as you wish to be forgiven.

9. **Keep thy home in order and good repair.** It brings contentment to your wife and praise from your neighbors.

10. **Honor God all the days of thy life** and your wife and children will rise up and honor you.

Okay, gentlemen, go out there and be the kind of husband God intended you to be. Don't disqualify yourself from the privilege of being married to a daughter of the King of the Universe.

Personal prayer:
Lord, you have given me your daughter to be my wife. Create in me the desire and ability to be worthy of her love. Help me to become the husband and father my wife and children need for me to be so that your name will be praised.

The Curse

One of the most fascinating stories in the Bible takes place early in the book of Genesis.

Adam and Eve are still in the Garden of Eden. The newness has worn off. They have been together a while. Fifty years? 100 years? Who knows? (They lived a long time.) No kids yet. Maybe it was boredom, but they suddenly take an unhealthy interest in the "forbidden fruit."

Of course, Lucifer's best salesman, the serpent, is there to close the deal.

Then God shows up and confronts them. After a couple rounds of "The Blame Game" (You know—Adam blames Eve, Eve blames the serpent ...), God pronounces judgment upon them. We call this "The Curse."

The effects of this curse are still present today, but they are so much more than labor pains or pulling weeds. If I were to boil down "The Curse" into non-theological terms, it would be that men will derive significance from their **work.** ("By the sweat of your brow you will eat your food" Genesis 3:19, NIV.) Women will derive their sense of satisfaction and meaning from their **relationships.** ("Your desire will be for your husband" Genesis 3:15, NIV.)

It is true that men tend to define themselves and derive the greatest personal satisfaction from their occupation. Esteem is based on accomplishment, being the best at what you do, vanquishing the enemy, or beating the competition. The warrior spirit. We lead with our professions. "Hi, my name is Tom. I'm an electrician." We want to gain recognition and acclaim for what we have done and respect from the men we ourselves respect.

Women tend to define themselves and derive their greatest sense of satisfaction from their relationships. "Hi, my name is Mary. I am John's wife, Bob's daughter, Jennifer's mom." They crave acceptance, love, and close personal friendships. They are constantly monitoring their relationships and are tuned in to emotional fluctuations in them. They love sacrificially and seek to be loved in the same way.

In today's world men still seek to be *respected* and women still seek to be *loved*.

Dr. Emerson Eggerichs wrote a book a few years ago called *Love & Respect*[1] in which he expounds on the Apostle Paul's teaching in the letter to the Ephesians. "Husbands ... each one of you also must love his wife as he loves himself, and the wife must respect her husband" (Ephesians 5:33, NIV).

Sounds simple enough. Besides, that is precisely what you want, right? But that is not always how it plays out, is it?

There are two problems here: One is that you tend to *give* what you *want* rather than what your partner *needs*. And two, if you do not get what you need, you tend not to give what your partner needs.

Let's take it a step further because the Scriptures imply that you should insert the word "unconditional"—unconditional love and unconditional respect!

Blame it on The Curse, but I think it is easier for women to love unconditionally and for men to respect unconditionally. That is normal, but that is not what Paul said to do. He tells men to *love* their wives *unconditionally* and for women to *respect* their husbands *unconditionally*.

Each is to do the thing that does *not* come naturally to them. That is much harder!

God always seems to be calling you to do what is "perfect" and "holy." There can be no room for "but he is not respectable" or "she is not lovable." No strings, no conditions.

I believe that if you *first* give your partner what he or she *needs*, he or she will respond by giving you what you need. **If you love your wife unconditionally, you will get respect back.** Gina will tell you that when she shows me unconditional respect (which I crave), I tend to respond more lovingly.

This is not an easy thing to do, but like anything else, if you are going to become good at it, you have to practice. Perhaps you cannot "undo" The Curse (Jesus has already done that), but you can minimize the impact of it in your spouse's life.

Men, go out there and love your wife unconditionally today.

Women, go out there and respect your husband unconditionally today.

Personal prayer:
Lord, help me to discern what it is my spouse truly needs, whether it is love, respect, or anything else, and give me a heart that is willing to give sacrificially. Give me the humility, commitment, and discipline to think of my spouse's needs before I think of my own.

Unconditional Respect

You may be familiar with the biblical concept of *agapé* love. It is Godly love. It is unconditional—no strings, no terms, no conditions, and no compromise. It is exclusive, and eternal. It is love that is constant, even if the person being loved has not behaved lovingly.

This kind of love cannot be earned, nor is it deserved. God is the only one who does it perfectly, and he has revealed that perfect love in Jesus. He loves us in spite of our unloveliness.

Paul the Apostle commands husbands to have this same kind of agapé love for their wives.

Everyone agree? (I can hear all the wives shouting, "Amen!") No problem. Not easy, but we get it.

Women desire love. It seems to come easily and naturally to them. They want more than anything else to love and be loved.

But, Paul does not end the sentence there. He commands wives to respect their husbands unconditionally as well. "[Husbands], each one of you also must love his wife as he loves himself, and the wife must respect her husband" (Ephesians 5:33, NIV).

Why did Paul phrase it in this way? Aren't wives supposed to *love* their husbands? Yes! But men do not resonate to being loved in the same way that women do.

Most men desire to be respected as much or more than being loved. It is easier for them to express respect to someone than it is to express love. They seem to resonate more with the idea of being respected by people whom they respect.

Someone may say, "My husband has not done anything to earn my respect," or, "He is not a very respectable man."

But that is not being "unconditional." How would a woman feel if her husband told her she had to *earn* his love?

Ephesians 5:33 is no accident or mistranslation of the Scriptures. Paul knew exactly what he was talking about. God always seems to call us to do that which is neither natural nor easy.

Here is the dilemma:

We do not have a problem saying, "Husbands, you should love your wives, even if she is being unloving, irresponsible, or mean." But we have difficulty saying, "Wives respect your husbands, even if he is an unbeliever, is being rude, insensitive, or just got fired."

In this scenario the husband has to love his wife, no matter what, but he also has to *earn* her respect! Do you see the problem? It looks as if the man is doing all the hard work.

If she is disrespectful to him, is he supposed to continue to love her unconditionally? Yes!

If he is unloving to her, is she supposed to continue to respect him? In all fairness, yes.

I didn't say it was easy.

If she is disrespectful, he responds unlovingly. If he is unloving, she responds disrespectfully.

Dr. Eggerichs, in his book *Love & Respect*[1], describes this process as a self-perpetuating "Crazy Cycle," which will eventually end in either misery or divorce. A ride on the **Crazy Cycle** leads to being unloving, which generates disrespect, which leads to more unloving responses ... ad infinitum!

One negative response will invite another from your spouse. It doesn't matter who starts it.

On the other hand, respect creates love, which leads to more respect. This is the **Energizing Cycle**. (If you are going to be on a cycle, this one is a lot more fun.)

When Gina first read this book several years ago, she didn't believe it could be true, so she decided to try an experiment—on me!

In order to prove Dr. Eggerichs wrong, she went out of her way to speak respectfully to me. (At that point in my life, I was neither very loving nor very respectable.) But, wouldn't you know it, I responded lovingly back to her. She couldn't believe it worked—every time!

Whose responsibility is it to break the cycle and turn it around in the other direction? *Yours!* Do not wait for your spouse to take the lead. It is *your* responsibility. Lay your ego down at the foot of the cross, and get started.

Unconditional love accompanied by unconditional respect has the power to break the cycle of hurt and bring about healing in your marriage. We did, and it made a huge difference.

I dare you to do the same.

Personal prayer:
(**Husbands**) Lord, help me to behave lovingly even when my wife is being disrespectful. Give me the insight to understand that her disrespect may be a response to me being unloving.

(**Wives**) Lord, help me to respond to my husband respectfully even when he does not deserve it. I realize that when I treat him respectfully, he is more likely to respond lovingly.

Husbands Lead,
Wives ... What?

Relax. Take a deep breath. Hold It ... Now let it go slowly. Do that one more time.

Okay, are you ready? Today we are going to talk about submission.

Stay calm. Don't freak out. We can get through this.

For you ladies out there, the good news is that submission is not just for women anymore. For you gentlemen, the bad news is that it never was just for women.

Okay, I've got some explaining to do.

The whole idea of submitting ourselves to someone else's power or authority, even for a brief period of time, is a challenge for Americans. We have not been subject to a monarch with the power of life and death over us for over two-and-a-half centuries.

We are proud pioneers—strong, tough, independent, and self-reliant. We humble ourselves to no one (rarely even to God).

I was curious about the root meaning of the word "submit," so I dusted off my old Latin vocabulary cards and discovered that the Latin word is ... "submitto." (Okay, that was not very helpful.)

It literally means "to send to help," or to be "under (sub) the mission (mitto = to send)." In other words, it is to place yourself under the leadership of someone else for the purpose of helping.

I think the most misunderstood part here is that it is a *voluntary* act. I place myself under someone's authority to accomplish a specific task. I do it voluntarily because I believe in the cause, the mission.

Guys, if you demand that your wife submit to your arbitrary and selfish demands based solely on your position as head of the household, you may get some begrudging compliance, but you will never get submission. That is what we call coercion.

This is not a matter of semantics. There is an important distinction here.

According to the Apostle Paul in Ephesians 5:22-33, her husband is the only authority, besides God, to whom a woman is called to submit. Paul also says in that passage that the husband must love his wife as he loves his own body—which means that he won't do anything to harm his wife.

Therefore, for a woman to willingly submit herself to her husband, she must have a reasonable expectation that he will protect and guide her. Before she can submit her will to his leadership, she must first buy into his vision for the task, for her, for them as a couple, and for the family.

God calls a man, first, to submit to him, before he attempts to lead anyone. If you have not submitted your will and your life to God, then do not expect your wife and children to be willing to submit to you.

A wife rarely has a problem submitting to her husband's leadership when he has:

- submitted himself to God,
- communicated his passionate vision to her and the children,
- served them by consistently meeting their needs, and
- protected them from destructive forces outside the family.

The real issue of a wife submitting to her husband is whether or not her husband has first submitted himself to God. If he takes care of his part, the other part is automatic.

Guys, here is where you get to make the first move. You should worry more about your relationship with God and your obedience to him, than about whether or not your wife is doing what you told her to do.

Now go out there and submit to one another … and God will lift you up.

Personal prayer:
Lord, the hardest task I have had to face is submitting my life, my will, and my ego to you. Forgive me when I try to claim them back as my own. May I become the kind of man and leader whom my wife will be willing to follow.

Eve

Eve: Hey! Wake up!

Adam: Huh?

Eve: Wake up, big guy! Who are you and what is this place?

Adam: Me? Adam, You ... I don't know who you are. Have we met?

Eve: (under her breath) Great! Just my luck, I get stuck alone in a zoo with a dumb jock.

(To Adam) Hey, Bohunk, is there anyone else around here I can have an intelligent conversation with, or am I stuck with monosyllabic responses from Tarzan, Jr.?

Adam: Now wait just a minute, lady! That's not fair. That was some pretty heavy-duty anesthetic God put me under. Sorry if I'm a little slow to gather my wits. I'm not a "morning guy."

Eve: You can't gather what you never had.

Adam: Hey!

Eve: I'm just sayin'. What's this?

Adam: Ouch! Don't poke me there. I feel like I just had a rib removed. I still don't know your name. I certainly didn't name you. I named everybody else and I would have remembered you. I've never seen anyone like you before.

Eve: I'm Eve. You're kind of cute, in a rugged, slightly off-kilter kind of way. I guess you'll have to do.

Adam: Thanks, I think.

Eve: What do you do for a living? Do you actually have a job or do you just sit around in your man-cave naming things?

Adam: Well, besides naming all the animals (I'm especially proud of "apteryx" and "platypus"), I tend the garden.

Eve: Good for you. Go fetch me that apple over there, Farm Boy, I'm hungry.

Adam: As you wish. (Note the obscure references to "The Princess Bride"[1])

- - - - - - - - -

Okay, so maybe that isn't *exactly* how it happened, but it does raise some interesting questions.

- How long were Adam and Eve married? 500 years? 700? 800?
- What do you give your wife for your 500th anniversary?
- What was their relationship like before they got kicked out of Eden? After?
- What do you do with thirty generations of grandchildren? That's a lot of birthdays!

Even though the Bible leaves a lot of gaps in the narrative, it is apparent that Adam knew immediately that Eve was different from everything else in all creation, and that she was spectacularly designed to match up with him (read Genesis 2: 21-25).

They were ideal for each other.

What would it be like to be married to the "ideal" man or woman? Someone who is perfect for you in every way? The one person in the whole world who is ideally suited for you?

I have good news and bad news. The good news—you *are* married to the ideal person! The bad news—you probably don't think you are.

Truthfully, you are potentially married to the ideal person, but you have to *make* it a reality.

Adam and Eve did not have any other options. They were stuck with each other. But you did have other options. You chose the person you did for very good reasons. But that does not mean that God was not involved in the process.

What were the odds of the two of you getting together in the first place? (Apparently, pretty good, right?) But think of all the thousands of big and small decisions in your lives that led you both to that particular place at that exact moment in time. Did you pick a winner, or does it sometimes seem as if you are married to a consolation prize?

In every sport I have ever seen, the winner is not determined until the very end of the competition. Many of the soccer matches in the World Cup soccer championship are decided in extra time. Maybe you need to give yourself and your spouse some "extra time" to become winners.

What can you do to hurry that process along in your less-than-perfect spouse?

- Pray for him or her daily,
- Work on your own attitude,
- Behave consistently,
- Renew your commitment daily,
- Live sacrificially,
- Love lavishly, even when it doesn't seem to be reciprocated,
- Respect and appreciate your spouse always.

These will go a long way toward turning your "ideal" mate into a Hall of Fame Spouse!

Your assignment is to write down *fifteen* things about your partner that makes him or her ideal for you. Then tell your partner how you *really* feel.

Personal prayer:
Lord, thank you for giving me an ideal spouse. I, too, came into this marriage incomplete and in need of grace to become an ideal mate myself. Help me to grow into the mate that my partner deserves.

Sanctuary

What do you think of when I say the word "sanctuary"? Safety? Peace? Quiet? A refuge from the storms of life? Or a place to hide or get away?

The Latin root word for sanctuary is *sanctus*, meaning "holy." Holy sites, such as churches, temples, mountaintops, and shrines, have always been considered special places, places where God resides. They are places that, if you can just get there in time, you will be safe; the "bad" guys cannot harm you. It is like an American embassy in a foreign country. An embassy is a small piece of America on foreign soil. It is a refuge.

The word *refuge* also has a Latin root meaning, "to flee again." It implies that in times of trouble we can go there and find safety and no one will harm us. It is a place (sometimes it only exists in our imagination) where we can escape from the turmoil of life and find peace. It is a place where we are accepted and can feel safe and relaxed.

When the Israelites conquered Canaan and occupied the land, God decreed that they were to designate six "cities of refuge." These were cities scattered around the country where someone who had accidentally killed a person could flee and be safe from retaliation by the victim's family—until he could come to trial. However, if he left the safety of the city of refuge, he was at risk. These cities of refuge were administered by the Levites, the priestly tribe, so that they would be seen as holy places and where there would be no political alliances (read Numbers 35:6-14).

As God designated the cities of refuge to be safe places for people, so he has designated our homes to be sanctuaries, as well.

We have all heard the old saying that "home is where the heart is." Unfortunately, when some people think of words like sanctuary, refuge, acceptance, peace, love, or harmony, "home" is not the concept that immediately comes to mind. Whether your personal experience of home and family was abuse and loneliness or joy, unity, and laughter, we all have a sense of how it is *supposed* to be.

I have an idealistic view of home and family. I believe home *should* be a sacred place. There *should* be honor, trust, mutual respect and fun. It should be a "home base."

This does not happen accidentally. It takes deliberate effort by a husband and wife who love, honor and deeply respect each other and who are each closely connected with their Creator.

Children can thrive in that environment. Only a home in which God is at the center (and the parents are committed and submitted to him and to each other) can hope to withstand the turmoil of life. When your children need a sanctuary, home should be the first place they look, because they are always welcome there!

Husbands and wives, begin today creating a sacred place of refuge for future generations, for your friends, neighbors, and strangers. May it always be said of us that "my house is God's house and it is your house, for when you are here, you are family and you are loved." You belong.

Personal prayer:
Lord, make my home a sanctuary for anyone who seeks refuge, rest, or peace. May I always be a safe person for others and my home a holy place where you dwell in our midst. Thank you for being my sanctuary.

Jaws

One of the greatest Hollywood productions of all time is "Jaws,"[1] the movie that made us think twice about swimming in the ocean. To this day when I am at the beach, I scan just beyond the breakers for shark fins.

Admit it. So do you.

And who can escape that haunting musical theme? Bah-dum. Bah-dum, bah-dum. I have even been known to scan the local swimming pool before jumping in, just to be safe.

In one of the scenes, Robert Shaw and Richard Dreyfuss are in the boat's cabin comparing scars from past diving injuries. "I got this from a moray eel." "I got this from a bull shark." "I got this one from a thresher shark."

Finally, Richard Dreyfuss points to his chest and says, "I got this one from Mary Ellen Moffatt. She broke my heart in second grade." That one trumped them all.

It is true that some wounds never completely heal. Long after the pain of the injury has subsided, the mental, emotional, and physical scars remain.

No matter how hard we try to get through life without getting our hearts broken, some carnage is inevitable.

John Eldredge wrote in his book, *Wild at Heart*², that we all enter adulthood with "arrows in our heart," put there by the ones we love the most.

Is it true that the more we care, the more likely we are to get hurt? Probably. If that is true, then, is the only way to keep from getting hurt not to care anymore? I certainly hope not, because that is a dangerous path to travel.

I knew a woman many years ago who was one of the most fear-stricken people I have ever met. She was often paralyzed by fear, literally becoming immobilized. After working on her fears for a long time, she recognized that she often experienced "a fear of the fear." She was afraid of being afraid.

It is this fear that keeps us from venturing outside of our comfort zones, especially in relationships. It is what prevents us from taking new risks and what keeps us stuck in old habits and patterns.

Physical scars are the legacy of a wound that has healed. Scars represent victory over adverse experience.

The scars we collect in life physically are what make us interesting as human beings. Each scar comes with a story, some funny, some sad. But it is our scars, our weaknesses, and our failures that make us human and relatable.

Wounds beg for healing and must be dealt with gently. Scars beg for storytelling and perhaps a little teasing and joviality.

Sometimes we gain respect for a person after hearing the story of how he or she overcame adversity, survived disaster, or beat insurmountable odds. Other times we gain friends by learning that they did the same dumb stuff we did.

Emotional wounds cut deeper, take longer to heal, and don't always leave a visible scar. A broken heart is a fragile thing and must be protected at all costs. Our most common response to a broken heart is to withdraw to a safe emotional place and say, "I will never let that happen again."

A heart in pain or that has become desensitized can only focus on its own hurt. It can neither see nor care about the pain in another's life. The problem is that a heart that has been shut down can no longer feel. "Isn't that the point?" you say. While it may be true that the goal is to prevent further heartbreak, a heart that *cannot* be hurt is a dangerous thing.

No one can guarantee that you will never be hurt again. But, your heart will not work properly if it is permanently locked away in a safe or encased in concrete. As we discussed in Marriage Minute #14, even scabs must eventually fall off! The remaining scar will be tender for a while, but needs the fresh air to continue to heal.

One of the most difficult things in life is to take your heart out of cold storage, rip the scabs off, and start feeling again. On the rare times in my life when I have actually done that, my heart started growing again and, like the Grinch, I was able to give and receive love. I was able to take the risk.

Let God heal your heart. Trust that the Maker of Hearts knows how to fix broken ones.

Jesus never stopped caring, never stopped loving, even though he died with a broken heart! All you have to do is take the risk.

Is it scary? **Yes!**
Will it hurt? **Probably.**
Is it worth it? **Oh, yes!**

Personal prayer:
Lord, heal my heart. I give you permission to rip off any scabs that prevent me from having a heart of flesh. Help me to see that your love is bigger than my fear! Never let my fear and hurt prevent me from caring for others.

Doofus

I am a doofus.

No, no, it's okay. I'm okay with being a doofus. I have been one for a long time. I proudly confess that I am not *just* a doofus, I am a Master Doofus! I hope someday to attain the status of "Doofus Extraordinaire"!

I am a well-intentioned doofus.

I am not often an idiot, except sometimes when I am driving. Rarely am I an insensitive clod, so I have made progress. But, in spite of my wife's best efforts to fix me, I will likely continue to be a doofus for some time to come.

The bad news is, your husband probably will, too.

Sometimes I am also a klutz. That is why I am not allowed to handle sharp objects in the kitchen or operate any power tool without supervision.

Sometimes I say the wrong things and I don't always listen very well, even though I pretend to.

You are probably thinking, "Wow, this guy needs help!" Well, yes, but mostly I need grace. I am not a high-maintenance guy, but I do require some routine upkeep. You know, change the oil and rotate the tires every 5000 miles.

Whether he is a rookie doofus, an apprentice, or an expert, I suspect that your husband struggles with many of these same issues. So pay attention to the warning lights on the dashboard, because he may not be very good at letting you know what he needs.

If he is not adept at articulating his needs or feelings, that does not mean he has none at all. He is not an emotionless brute. Have you ever watched him during football season? That's passion! If we can just re-direct that energy and get him to be that fanatical about you!

As a man, he tends to avoid what makes him uncomfortable (sounds like a good definition of doofus to me). Being vulnerable is definitely uncomfortable, but most men really do want to please their spouse. So, if your husband approaches you with his heart in his hands, please be gentle. It is a love offering.

Men, it is very important to remember that you are no longer who you were. Leave the past behind. Don't get too comfortable or proud of who you are now, because God is not done growing you. You are still under construction.

Focus on the man God wants you to become! Never quit. Never give up.

Ladies, is your husband ever going to be cured of being a doofus? Probably not. No matter how amazing a person he becomes, in all likelihood, there will continue to be some residual doofusness (doofosity?) in him. But, he loves you and needs for you to respect and love him in return.

Extend grace to him. God is still growing him into the man that he is destined to be—and the man that you need him to be.

Personal Prayer:

(Men) Lord, help me not to be a doofus, or help me come to terms with my weaknesses. I don't care how you change me, as long as you and my wife are proud of me. Use my weakness to bring glory to you.

(Women) Lord, give me strength to endure and the eyes to see him as you do—a warrior who would sacrifice himself to protect me and the kids and who desires to serve his God.

Tigger and Eeyore

When my boys were young, our whole family loved Winnie the Pooh.[1] We would read the books and watch the movies and cartoons. We even sang the songs. It became part of our family culture. Over the years my memory has become a lot like Pooh Bear's, but I still enjoy the characters.

My favorites are Tigger and Eeyore.

I like Tigger because he has a huge amount of energy and he can bounce high in the sky. I used to dream of that. He is always positive and excited about life. "The wonderful thing about Tiggers is I'm the only one!" He exudes self-confidence. That often gets him in over his head, but he can rebound faster than anyone. He has his short-comings and fears, but who wouldn't be a little frightened of *heffalumps and woozels*, not to mention those ferocious *jagulars*? In short, he is most of the things I am not.

Eeyore, on the other hand, I can really identify with. He is the epitome of doom and gloom. His most famous line is, "Hunh, it's prob'ly gonna rain." He always expects the worst, and is rarely disappointed. Even when things eventually work out, as they always do, Eeyore is still depressed, still a pessimist. I don't think I am that bad, but I can certainly see where he is coming from.

If you are a "Tigger" and are married to someone who is like Eeyore—what were you thinking?

No, I'm kidding. But whether you are the Tigger or the Eeyore in the relationship, you are going to have some challenges.

Why would Tigger and Eeyore become friends in the first place? It is true that opposites *do* attract, but only initially. If you are a high-energy, chaotic Tigger, you can easily be attracted to Eeyore's stable, down-to-earth demeanor. And you Eeyores out there will find Tigger's bubbly personality and exuberant enthusiasm exciting.

We unconsciously tend to look for someone who will balance us out and take up the slack for our own deficiencies.

After five to ten years of marriage, however, this attractive difference can become annoying and irritating. In the field of magnetism, polar opposites are attracted to each other. That can also happen in marriages. But, those characteristics we initially find cute or attractive gradually become points of conflict.

Her need for structure and tidiness become oppressive compulsivity. "I have checked the stove three times and it is still off."

His "free spirit" becomes irresponsibility and unpredictability. "When are you going to grow up and start taking responsibility?"

If that's where you find yourself, listen up!

1. Do not forget why you were attracted to and married this person in the first place.
2. Cherish and appreciate him or her.
3. Recognize and accept him or her for the difference he/she has made in your life.
4. Do not try to change your partner to be more like you. You won't like it.

5. Adapt to each other's needs. Speed up to keep up, or slow down so he/she can keep up.
6. Both of you are constantly changing, so be patient.
7. Love him or her anyway!

Enjoy the adventure, Tigger!

And, Eeyore, it might *not* rain.

Personal prayer:
Lord, thank you for my amazing spouse and how well we complement each other. Help us to always accept and appreciate the differences that make us compatible. Give us blind eyes and deaf ears to those differences we find annoying. Thank you for filling us with joy and grace.

Earning Points vs. Keeping Score

If a man brings his wife a rose, she is delighted with him, and gives him one point. Fair enough. If he brings her twelve roses, he also gets one point.

Wait. What? That doesn't sound right. It should be *at least* twelve points.

Nope, it's just one point.

If he washes *and* dries the dishes, he gets one point. If he did something nice yesterday, but not today, he gets no points, right?

Wrong again. He gets *minus* one point. If he complains about it, he gets minus five points.

In a man's mind, if he makes any effort at all, he should get a great deal of credit for it.

If he asks, "Hey, how is your mother doing? Let me say hello to her on the phone." Ding, ding, ding, ding! 100 points! She is delighted!

Mark Gungor is a pastor from Green Bay, Wisconsin, who conducts a wonderful marriage seminar that he calls, "Laugh Your Way to a Better Marriage."[1] He has a very humorous way of exposing biblical truth and how it applies to modern marriages. He pokes fun at himself, his marriage, gender differences, and sexuality, and leaves the audience laughing and better informed.

One of the areas that he makes fun of is how men and women "earn points" from each other. As you would expect, men and women score behavior very differently.

Men are more generous in giving their wives points. If his wife shows up and intervenes when a child is crying or has a smelly diaper, she earns 100,000 points, easily!

If he gets lucky tonight after the kids are asleep—one million points!

Whether he earns one hundred thousand points or just two points, a man enjoys delighting his wife.

The only problem that comes up is when one or both begin to "keep score."

Keeping score can cause damage to a marriage. It changes the focus of the relationship. It introduces a sense of competition between two people who should not be competing, but cooperating. It creates a system that degrades from counting blessings to keeping track of offenses.

The Apostle Paul says that "[love] is not easily angered, it keeps no record of wrongs" (1 Corinthians 13:5, NIV). Keeping score can lead to bad feelings, a build-up of resentment, and a sense of unfairness or mistreatment in the relationship.

Love is not concerned about who has more points, or how many times you have offended me this week, or that you had two cookies and I had only one.

Love is concerned with

- How can I serve you?
- How can I lift you up and encourage you?
- How can I help you along the way in your walk with God?
- How can I help you become the person God wants you to be?
- How can I help you accomplish your dreams and goals?

I bet that kind of talk will get you some major points. Whether you get a lot of points or just one, this is not a competition between you and your spouse. Nor is it about scoring more points than any other husband or wife at work.

If Gina and I kept track of points, I would be millions of points in the RED! No matter what accounting method you use, you cannot collect points fast enough to repay a debt of love.

But scoring points is all about the value that you bring to the relationship, and it's kind of fun!

So, how many points do you have to get to have a happy marriage? That's the wrong question.

The correct question is, "What will it *cost* you to have a great marriage?"

Everything! You cannot pay for a great marriage with money, chocolates, or imaginary points, because it's free. But it will cost you everything.

Now go out there and make your partner's eyes light up with delight when you enter the room. You just might earn a bunch of points.

Personal prayer:

Lord, no amount of money or effort can ever repay the debt of love I owe to you and to my spouse. Thank for your grace and mercy. May I always extend the same grace and mercy to everyone who comes into my life—without keeping score.

Captain Crabby

When my youngest son was small, he had a T-shirt with a cartoon crab on the front. Blazoned across his chest was the name "Captain Crabby." He proudly wore that shirt for two or three years, not realizing that we chose the shirt because it described his personality so well—crabby.

He definitely lived up to it.

I have never known a four-year-old kid who had such a negative world view. He was a committed contrarian. Whatever our view was, he would take the opposite side. He would debate and argue and it didn't seem to matter which side he took.

I used to joke with him about being the only person I knew who refused to take "yes" for an answer. He and his brother could agree on something and still argue about it!

To his credit, he has outgrown his negative, contrary approach to life and is now much more fun to be around. It was tough for a few years, wondering if he was ever going to overcome his negative beliefs and attitudes. (He must have gotten it from one of his uncles!)

Do you know people who are so negative, so dismal that they are difficult to be around? It is not easy to maintain a positive attitude around such people. Sometimes you feel like taking a shower for fear that you might catch whatever it is they have.

You might have grown up in a family that was negative, hostile, or dysfunctional and that is all you have ever known.

What if a crabby person lives in your house? There are many reasons for someone to be negative, depressed, or crabby.

1. **If it is due to a psychological disorder**, get counseling and/ or medication.
2. **If it is due to physical pain or medical issues**, get proper treatment. Do *not* let it go untreated.
3. **If it is due to past trauma or abuse from childhood**, get help!
4. **If it is due to grief or loss**, be patient. Time will heal most of it. Get support and comfort from others who have suffered similar losses.
5. **If it is the result of personal failure or low self-esteem**, build that person up. (See below.)
6. **If it is due to bad emotional habits or a certain personality type that may be prone to negativity**, an "attitude adjustment" may be in order. Learn new ways of thinking and behaving.

What do you do if the most negative person in your life is your spouse?

A. Overwhelm his or her negativity with praise and appreciation.
B. Be constantly encouraging and uplifting.
C. Never add to the negative pile. "Do not let any unwholesome talk come out of your mouths" (Ephesians 4:29, NIV).
D. Love this person into healthiness. Love is still the most powerful force in the universe. It may take some time, but light is more powerful than darkness, and love is more powerful than crabbiness.

E. Make sure that every encounter is a positive experience, or ends on a positive note. Positive interactions have a profound and long-lasting effect.

F. Laugh a lot. Laughter is more powerful than crabbiness. Do not be overcome by crabbiness, but overcome crabbiness with laughter (Romans 12:21). While that might not be a direct quote, I am sure that is what the Apostle Paul really intended to say.

G. Some people love anything sour, but "sour" makes my whole body pucker. Add a lot of sweetener to the relationship.

Now, go out there and conquer crabbiness with love.

Personal prayer:
Lord, some enemies may be vanquished by sword and others by words, but you have conquered my heart with your love. Help me to be able to overcome negativity, fear, anxiety, and discouragement with massive doses of love.

Natural Disasters

It seems as if there have been a lot of natural disasters in the last few years—unusually destructive hurricanes, unseasonal snowstorms, earthquakes, floods, tornados, tsunamis, and wildfires.

Regardless of what you may believe about global climate change, the loss of property and life has been astronomical in the last decade or so. In the case of the tsunami in Japan a few years ago, it may be decades before we know the full scope and impact of the disaster.

I am fascinated by the stories of people who managed to survive such devastation—real life stories of courage, heroism, determination, and miraculous rescues. Their stories are horrifying and inspiring at the same time.

Question: What is the difference between a "natural climatic event" and a "natural disaster"?

Californians survive earthquakes all the time because they are prepared for them, even with no warning. My friend in Orlando, Florida, had his fence blown down four times in one year by four different hurricanes blowing from four different directions, but it was *not* a disaster.

An event such as a tornado, earthquake, or tsunami, no matter how big, that causes little or no damage to property or loss of human life, is not deemed a disaster and may not even make the news.

The two key elements to minimizing the impact of a geologic or climatic event and preventing disaster are **advance warning** and **preparation**. How much warning and time people had, and how well prepared they were—can make the difference between life and death.

Not surprisingly, this is true in marriages as well.

I have been amazed by how well some couples handle difficult life events and how devastating the same events can be to other couples.

Some couples bounce back relatively quickly after losing everything. Other couples wind up getting divorced after experiencing what seemed to me to be minor setbacks or disappointments.

I have discovered that there are four distinct spikes in the divorce rate. Each is preceded by a normal developmental event in the life of the couple. Couples who bail out after one, two, or three years never really gave marriage a chance, so I don't count them.

Spike #1 is at seven to ten years. This is what used to be known as "The Seven-Year Itch."

The developmental crisis that most often precedes this first spike is the massive invasion of human life forms commonly known as "children." Having a child changes almost everything about the marriage relationship and some couples never recover their former closeness and intimacy.

Spike #2 occurs somewhere around fifteen to twenty years.

The "crisis"—teenagers in the house. This is a daunting challenge for any family! Enough said.

Spike #3 takes place at twenty-five to thirty years of marriage.

This usually corresponds to the emptying of the nest. After thirty years of praying for peace and quiet, you now find yourself bored and lonely. Didn't expect that, did you?

Spike #4 occurs at forty+ years.

This is more of a "bump" than a spike; but is significant, nonetheless. It is connected with retirement and/or declining energy, resources, and health. After spending forty years being apart fifty to sixty hours per week because of a career, being together full-time can be an unexpected source of stress. The effects of drift (see MM #8) are most evident here.

So, approximately every ten years you will enter a new developmental stage in your marriage that will require new adaptation and skills.

Each of these stages represents a new and previously un-encountered challenge, and each requires a completely new set of coping strategies.

Any crisis will offer you the opportunity to change and grow, but these four developmental stages are normal and predictable and you *can* prepare for them.

There are other events that you may encounter along the way that will severely test your marriage, such as loss of a child, loss of employment, infidelity, severe injury or illness.

How do you survive these challenges?

- **Determine to grow.** Every crisis in life necessitates a choice—choose to grow and move forward, OR refuse to adapt (just quit). Quitting equals death for the relationship.
- **Prepare.** You know these events are coming and you know *when* they are coming. Unless you stamp "Return to Sender" on your three-year old's forehead, in ten years she *will* become a teenager! *Sooner* if she has her way.
- **Keep talking.** Communication is the key to growth. It is not easy to do that during a crisis, but you have to "up your game" if you want to overcome each challenge. You don't survive a tsunami by clinging to your favorite pool floatie. More extreme measures are required.
- **Get a tune-up!** Would your car run properly if you only tuned it up every ten years? Talk to a mentor couple or visit with a good marriage counselor. Get an annual check-up.
- **Pray!** Get prayed up; arm yourself spiritually. Don't wait until the boat is sinking to start looking for a life preserver.

Now get out there and don't let a natural event become a disaster! Keep growing.

Personal prayer:
Lord, help me to navigate the growth challenges of life with faith, preparation, wisdom, and determination. Help me to learn the lessons that you have embedded in such opportunities—and keep me growing.

Marriage Minute #54

The Gift You Give Yourself

I love serving people and I love giving gifts to people.

I love the first section of *The Fellowship of the Ring*[1] when Bilbo Baggins throws a party for his "eleventy-first" birthday and gives a gift to everyone who attends. One year in my 20s I gave my good friend, Rich, a new softball glove for *my* birthday. His fielding at second base improved so much that I considered it a gift to myself and the whole team.

Giving gifts (and receiving them) brings us so much joy and is so meaningful that Dr. Gary Chapman (*The Five Love Languages*[2]) believes it to be a profound way that we express love to each other.

But giving a gift to ourselves seems very selfish, unless that gift is FORGIVENESS.

I don't know about you, but the person I have the hardest time forgiving is me. I find that forgiving others is not that difficult, primarily because my memory is so bad. I am especially adept at not being able to remember negative things others have said about me or done to me.

Every morning I wake up and God has apparently wiped my hard drive while I slept and rebooted it. "Tabula rasa," blank slate, emptiness. **Thank you, Lord!**

The ability to forget slights and offenses is a huge blessing when it comes to forgiving. It is very difficult to bear a grudge or feel resentment over something too insignificant to remember.

This issue of forgiveness was so difficult for the Apostle Peter that he asked Jesus how many times he had to forgive his brother who offended him—"as many as seven times?" (Matthew 18:21-22, ESV) Jewish tradition required three times, so he felt he was being very generous.

He was aghast when Jesus said 490 times (70 x 7). What Peter did not understand was that if you forgive someone 490 times and then punch him after the 491st time, **you have not forgiven him even once!** If you have truly forgiven your brother, you have set the timer back to zero. If he offends you again, it will be the *first* time.

So, the real answer to how many times I have to forgive my brother is … *every* time. An additional benefit is that you don't have to keep track of how many more times your brother can offend you! The good news is that you only have to forgive someone *one* time—*this* time. That's all there is to forgive—one offense, one mistake.

Clean slate. Keep starting over at 1 and you will never get to 2, let alone 490.

It is usually easier to forgive offenses from strangers or people we barely know than it is to forgive people with whom we have an intimate relationship. This is because we have much higher expectations of those we love and care about, because they have the power to hurt and disappoint us more deeply.

The ability to forgive yourself and your partner is absolutely necessary for a healthy marriage.

Unforgiven hurt is one of the biggest destroyers of intimacy in marriage. That hurt can turn into bitterness and resentment over time. It can fester and poison our minds and hearts.

Forgiving your partner daily may or may not be a big deal to him or her, but it will make a huge difference to you. If you forgive your spouse, you are no longer "bound up" emotionally by him or her. (Think of being handcuffed to someone you don't like.)

Non-forgiveness allows other people to have emotional control over you, without being present or even alive.

Forgiveness frees you to love and serve. There is no carry-over of unfinished business from one day to the next.

What a gift to you and your mate!

Have you confessed your failure?
Have you repented/changed/grown?
Do you really *want* to be forgiven?
Have you asked God for forgiveness?
If yes, then God has forgiven you!
If God can forgive you, why can't you?

By the way, you deserve to be forgiven. Don't tell me that you can never forgive yourself for _____!

Do not oppose God here. That would look too much like spiritual arrogance. Your failure is not bigger than God's ability and willingness to forgive you.

Go on … do yourself a favor. Give yourself the gift of forgiveness. Forgive yourself and your partner daily and see what a difference it makes.

Jerry Shipp

Personal prayer:
Lord, you have forgiven me lavishly at great expense to yourself. Help me to forgive myself and my partner as freely as you have forgiven me.

Adam and Eve Redux

This is our last Marriage Minute. I hope you have enjoyed reading them and have gotten some practical help for your marriage.

I have made a lot of biblical references, but this has deliberately *not* been a Bible study. I will save that for the Bible scholars. But it has been fun to speculate and try to fill in some gaps.

We began with Adam and Eve, and it seems only fitting to end with them talking about their life together, their struggles, and the God who made them.

I can just hear Adam and Eve having a conversation on their 800th anniversary that may have gone something like this:

Eve: Adam?

Adam: Hmm?

Eve: Adam!!

Adam: What!?

Eve: Adam, do you still love me?

Adam: You're kidding, right?

Eve: I'm serious! Do you still love me?

Adam: Of course I still love you. Now that all our great, great, great, great, great, great, great ... great-grandchildren have finally moved out of the spare bedroom, you're all I've got.

Eve: Do you think I'm still cute? I feel so ... old.

Adam: Eve, you are 830 years old! You are the oldest woman in the whole world.
Didn't we just have this discussion seventy-five or eighty years ago?

Eve: Waaah! You hate me!

Adam: I'm sorry. I'm sorry. I didn't mean it.

(Three days later Eve stops crying.)

Adam: You are the cutest 830 year-old woman I have ever known. In fact, you don't look a day over 500.

Eve: Really? Thank you.
Adam, why did God put us together?

Adam: You mean besides my being lonely and all? Well, I have been thinking about that ever since we got kicked out the Garden.

Before you and I met, God and I were close, I mean REALLY close. It was like there were no barriers between us. But, when we disobeyed God and ate the fruit that he told us not to eat, everything changed. You were there; didn't you feel it, too?

Eve: Yes. It was like I couldn't feel his presence anymore. It felt as if something was in the way.

Adam: Exactly. That is what I miss the most. Since then, the relationship between you and me is the closest thing to the intimacy we once had with God. I think he wanted us to have a reminder of what it was like to be one with another.

Well, they *could* have had that discussion. The point is obvious. When we do it right, marriage is the closest thing on earth to a complete, intimate, restored relationship with God—no barriers, no distance, no misunderstanding, just LOVE.

If we remove God and cheapen marriage or corrupt it, it will become the most painful, disappointing, and devastating thing we can experience. Two broken hearts and two broken lives. That sounds a little like how God must have felt when we (not just Adam and Eve) rejected him.

Marriage is a sacred relationship, created by God to meet our physical, emotional, relational, and social needs in ways that no other relationship can.

Grow it. Strengthen it. Cherish it.

Now go out there and love your spouse the way God intended.

Personal prayer:
Lord, may our lives and our marriages be a beacon of light in a dark and discouraged world. May we always, in everything we do, bring glory and honor to you. Thank you for creating marriage as an earthly example of what an intimate relationship with you is like.

Notes

Chapter 3

1. Felder, Don (music), Frey, Glenn and Henley, Don (lyrics). *Hotel California*. Label: Asylum. Perf. Eagles. 1976. Album.

Chapter 5

1. *50 First Dates*. Dir. Peter Segal. Perf. Adam Sandler, Drew Barrymore. Columbia Pictures, Happy Madison Productions. 2004. Film.

Chapter 6

1. *In God's Kitchen*. Source unknown. 2013. Editorial Cartoon.

Chapter 12

1. A. Nonymous. "Five Deadly Words Used By a Woman." Source unknown. 2013. Web.
2. Gray, John. *Men Are from Mars, Women Are from Venus*. New York, NY: Harper Collins, 1992. Print.

Chapter 13

1. *Despicable Me*. Dir. Pierre Coffin and Chris Renaud. Story by Sergio Pablos. Perf. Steve Carrell, et al. Universal Pictures and Illumination Entertainment. 2010. Animation.
2. Zaret, Hy and North, Alex. *Unchained Melody*. Perf. Righteous Brothers. 1965.
3. Cetera, Peter and Foster, David. *You're the Inspiration*. Perf. Chicago. Label: Full Moon/Warner Bros. 1984.
4. Parton, Dolly. *I Will Always Love You*. Label: RCA Nashville. Perf. Whitney Houston. 1992.

Chapter 15

1. "Darmok." *Star Trek: Next Generation.* Created by Gene Roddenberry. Perf. Patrick Stewart. Season 5, Episode 2. September 9, 1991. Television.

Chapter 17

1. Carnegie, Dale. *How to Win Friends and Influence People.* New York, NY: Simon & Schuster, 1936, 1981. 4. Print.

Chapter 18

1. *Godzilla.* Dir. Ishiro Honda. Toho Company, Ltd. 1954. Film.

Chapter 22

1. *Get Smart.* Creators: Mel Brooks, Buck Henry. Perf. Don Adams, Barbara Feldon, Edward Platt. 1965-1970. NBC, CBS. Television.

Chapter 24

1. Covey, Steven R. *The 7 Habits of Highly Successful People.* New York, NY: Simon & Schuster. 1989. Print.
2. Maxwell, John C. *Everyone Communicates, Few Connect.* Nashville, TN: Thomas Nelson. 2010. Print.
3. Adams, Scott. *7 Years of Highly Defective People.* Kansas City, MO: Andrews McMeel Publishing. 1997. Print.
4. Arp, Dave & Claudia. *52 Dates for You and Your Mate.* Nashville, TN: Thomas Nelson. 1993. Print.

Chapter 25

1. Burroughs, Edgar Rice. *Tarzan of the Apes.* Chicago, IL: A.C. McClurg. 1914. Print.

Chapter 26
1.   Kipling, Rudyard. "The Elephant's Child" in *Just So Stories*. London: Macmillan & Co., 1902. Print. Perf. Jack Nicholson and Bobby McFerrin. Label: Windham Hill. 1987. Recording.

Chapter 27
1.   Geisel, Theodor (Dr. Seuss). *The Cat in the Hat*. New York: Random House. 1957. Print.
2.   Geisel, T. *Yertle the Turtle*. New York: Random House. 1958. Print.
3.   Geisel, T. *Green Eggs and Ham*. New York: Random House. 1960. Print.
4.   Geisel, T. *On Beyond Zebra*. New York: Random House. 1955. Print.
5.   Geisel, T. *How the Grinch Stole Christmas*. New York: Random House. 1957. Print. Dir. Charles M. Jones, Ben Washam. Narr. Boris Karloff. Author Dr. Seuss. 1966. Animated film.

Chapter 28
1.   Coughlin, Paul. *No More Christian Nice Guy*. Minneapolis, MN: Bethany House, 2005. 83. Print.

Chapter 32
1.   *True Lies*. Dir. James Cameron. Perf. Arnold Schwarzeneggar, Jamie Lee Curtis. Twentieth Century Fox. 1994. Film.

Chapter 33
1.   Doyle, Sir Arthur Conan. Sherlock Holmes first appears in print in *A Study in Scarlet*. London: Beeton's Christmas Annual, 1887. Print.
2.   Gungor, Mark. *Laugh Your Way to a Better Marriage*. (Full Seminar) Green Bay, WI: Crown Comedy. 2007. DVD.
3.   DeAngelis, Barbara. *What Women Want Men to Know*. New York, NY: Hyperion Books, 2001. Print.

Chapter 37
1. *Pepé Le Pew.* Created by Chuck Jones, Michael Maltese. Perf. Mel Blanc, et al. Looney Toons. 1945. Animation.
2. Thompson, Frances. *The Hound of Heaven.* Published in *The Oxford Book of English Mystical Verse,* Nicholson and Lee, eds. Oxford: The Clarendon Press, 1917. Print.

Chapter 38
1. *Snow White and the Seven Dwarfs.* Dir. David Hand. Auth. Jacob and Wilhelm Grimm. Walt Disney. 1937. Animated Film.
2. *Sleeping Beauty.* Dir. Clyde Geronimi. Auth. Charles Perrault. Walt Disney. 1959. Animated Film.

Chapter 39
1. Eldredge, John. *Wild at Heart.* Nashville, TN: Thomas Nelson, 2001. Print.

Chapter 40
1. Shipp, Glover H. *Ten Commandments for Couples.* Joplin, MO: College Press Publishing Co., 2002. 3-90. Print.

Chapter 41
1. Shipp, G. Op. cit. 98-99.
2. Eggerichs, Emerson. *Love & Respect.* Brentwood, TN: Integrity Publishers, 2004. Print.

Chapter 42
1. Shipp, G. Op. cit. 99-100.

Chapter 43
1. Eggerichs, E. Op. cit.

Chapter 44

1.   Eggerichs, E. Op, cit.

Chapter 46

1.   *The Princess Bride.* Dir. Rob Reiner. Screenplay by
      William Goldman (Adapted from his book) ACT III
      Communications/20th Century Fox. 1987. Film.

Chapter 48

1.   *Jaws.* Dir. Steven Spielberg. Perf. Roy Scheider, Richard
      Dreyfuss, Robert Shaw. Music John Williams. Universal
      Pictures. 1975. Film.
2.   Eldredge, J. Op. cit.

Chapter 50

1.   A.A. Milne, *When We Were Very Young.* London: Methuen &
      Co. 1924. Print.

Chapter 51

1.   Gungor, M. Op. cit.

Chapter 54

1.   Tolkien, J.R.R. *The Lord of the Rings.* United Kingdom: George
      Allen & Unwin Ltd. 1954. Print.
2.   Chapman, Gary. *The Five Love Languages.* Chicago, IL:
      Northfield Publishing, 1992, 1995. Print.

Printed in the United States
By Bookmasters